A Snowman's Family Album Quilt

A Snowman's Family Album Quilt

MARY M. COVEY

Martingale
& COMPANY

BOTHELL, WASHINGTON

Credits

President . . . . Nancy J. Martin
CEO . . . . Daniel J. Martin
Publisher . . . . Jane Hamada
Editorial Director . . . . Mary V. Green
Editorial Project Manager . . . . Tina Cook
Technical Editor . . . . Jane Townswick
Copy Editor . . . . Ellen Balstad
Design and Production Manager . . . . Stan Green
Illustrator . . . . Robin Strobel
Photographer . . . . Brent Kane
Cover and Text Design . . . . Magrit Baurecht

Martingale
& C O M P A N Y

That
Patchwork
Place®

That Patchwork Place is an imprint
of Martingale & Company.

A Snowman's Family Album Quilt
© 2000 by Mary M. Covey

Martingale & Company
PO Box 118
Bothell, WA 98041-0118 USA
www.patchwork.com

Printed in China
05 04 03 02 01 00   6 5 4 3 2 1

Library of Congress Cataloging-in-Publication Data

Covey, Mary M.
    A snowman's family album quilt / Mary M. Covey.
      p. cm.
    ISBN 1-56477-318-3
     1. Patchwork—Patterns. 2. Appliqué—Patterns.
     3. Patchwork quilts. 4. Snowmen in art.
    I. Title.
    TT835 .C694 2000
    746.46'041—dc21   00-033932

Mission Statement

We are dedicated to providing quality products and
service by working together to inspire creativity
and to enrich the lives we touch.

Dedication

To my husband, John, who encouraged me to develop my snowman idea. He believes in me even when I doubt myself.

To my daughter, Kristi, and my son, Michael, who are a constant source of encouragement and delight, and who are both very talented in their own right.

Acknowledgments

With thanks and appreciation to: Jane Green, for graciously helping me test block instructions; and Connie Crawley, a loyal and talented friend whose generous support was always available. She taught me to think "bright."

Contents

Introduction

Every quilter I know is a busy person. Quilters are talented people who work hard to maintain households, hold full- and part-time jobs outside the home, take children to various school and sporting events, do volunteer work, and so on, and so on, and so on. At one time or another, they have all had hobbies that they worked into their busy schedules. Two of my friends, Nancy and Jane, did china painting; my sister-in-law, Shirley, did ceramics; and another friend, Connie, did crafts. My own hobby was photography. But one by one, we each discovered quilting. And one by one, our other hobbies fell by the wayside as quilting completely took over any and all of our spare time.

My family was certainly relieved when I took an interest in something other than taking pictures of them. At every possible photo opportunity, I was there with my camera in hand—baseball games, birthday celebrations, school plays, vacation Bible school, skiing trips, the birth of kittens—even a trip to the backyard was enough for me to start shooting photos! And what good are photographs of such marvelous events unless you place them in a family album for viewing? Every year we added new snapshots—the arrival of Kristi's new baby brother; searches in plump, padded snowsuits for the perfect Christmas tree; visits to the pumpkin patch; spring break; skiing and fishing trips; Papa's gold watch presented at retirement. We had numerous volumes filled with photos celebrating family memories. At every gathering of friends and family, we pulled out the albums and enjoyed reminiscing.

During one of these times, I ran across a photo of Kristi and Michael that had been taken sometime during the first week we lived in our new house. They had taken their evening baths and were clearly ready for bed. Kristi was sitting on the couch, reading the book *Frosty the Snowman* to her little brother. From that small photo taken twenty years ago, an idea began to form in my mind.

If a snowman had a family album, what kinds of pictures would be in it? Maybe his album would hold some of the very same treasures that ours did. With that in mind, I picked some of the most memorable times from our family's history and made the snowman's history, too. *A Snowman's Family Album Quilt* is a whimsical look at the family portraits of a favorite snowman, which were made with fun and lightheartedness. I have named each of the quilt blocks as if I were labeling pictures in my own family's album.

Have fun making the snowman quilt (as it is lovingly referred to at our house), and use your imagination. Incorporate some of your own family's history into the quilt, or give your blocks different titles from family events or vacations, such as "Spring Break" or "First Ski Trip."

Before starting to make a quilt, read through all of the instructions for that project. This will help you get an idea of the complete process for that particular quilt, and there will be no surprises. The snowman quilt has lots of room for embellishments, so you may add or delete as many or as few as you wish. This will guarantee that each quilt you make will be as individual as you are.

Mary

General Directions

Fabric Selection

Who knows why certain fabrics catch our attention. Maybe it's the pattern that attracts us, or the color. We are each attracted to fabric in different ways. The choices available to us can sometimes be overwhelming. But whether you shop for new fabric for the projects in this book, or pull from your own fabric stash, here are a few guidelines to remember.

Content, Care, and Style

Select high-quality, 100 percent–cotton fabrics. They hold their shape well and are easy to handle. Cotton blends can be more difficult to stitch and press. (Sometimes, however, a cotton blend is worth a little extra effort if it is the perfect fabric for your quilt.)

Yardage requirements are provided for all of the projects in this book and are based on 42" of usable fabric after preshrinking. Some quilts call for an assortment of scraps. If you have access to scraps, feel free to use them and purchase only those fabrics you need to complete the quilt you are making.

Wash all fabrics to test for colorfastness. Remove the excess dyes from the fabrics and preshrink them. Make sure to wash dark and light colors separately so that the dyes from the dark colors will not run onto light fabrics. Some fabrics may require several rinses to eliminate the excess dyes. Also, use warm water and a mild laundry soap with no bleach additives to wash your fabrics. You can also use soaps that are specifically made for washing quilts and that are available in quilt shops or fabric stores. Once you wash and preshrink your fabrics, press them so that you can cut out the pieces for a quilt accurately.

Color is the factor that will make a quilt sparkle. Work with colors you like very much and that are alike in feeling. Many of the projects in this book feature clear, bright colors, such as the six major colors of the color wheel: red, yellow, blue, green, orange, and violet. To highlight a color, select its complementary color (the color directly across from it as shown on the color wheel below) to place next to it. Any two complementary colors will make each other stronger, such as blue and orange or yellow and violet.

Once you've selected your basic color palette, add fabrics that are lighter and darker to each color group. Try not to use plain white or off-white. Instead, opt for tone-on-tone or white-on-white prints. These will add dimension to your project. Use a variety of designs, textures, and styles of fabric. Feel free to experiment. And always trust your instincts.

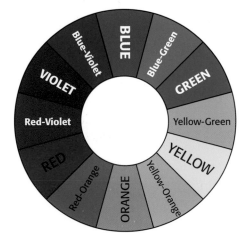

Grain Lines

I'd like to include a word about grain lines: the lengthwise grain runs parallel to the selvage edges of fabric and has very little stretch. The crosswise grain runs from selvage to selvage and has some give to it. True bias runs at a 45° angle to the lengthwise and crosswise grain lines.

When rotary cutting fabric, cut striped fabric along the crosswise grain. Cut shapes like squares and rectangles on the lengthwise and crosswise grains. That way, when you sew these pieces back together, the threads will lie naturally, as the fabric was originally woven. This will prevent stretching and buckling in a quilt top. In appliqué, as long as the background is on the lengthwise and crosswise grains, the pieces being appliquéd will not become distorted.

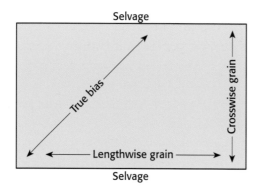

Yardage

The amounts of yardage provided in the materials lists for each project are ample. You may have an extra strip or two of fabric, and some irregularly sized scraps left over when only a single or a few appliqué pieces need to be cut from the fabric. Save these scraps and keep them on hand for other projects in the book.

Tools and Equipment

The right tools and equipment are essential for any job, and quilting is no different. Most of the things needed for quilting are general sewing tools that you probably already own. If you need to purchase any new equipment, invest in the best quality that you can afford. It is much more enjoyable to work when you use equipment that consistently produces good results.

Rotary Cutters, Mats, and Rulers

For quick and accurate rotary cutting, you will need a rotary cutter, cutting mat, and clear acrylic

rulers in a variety of sizes. A 6" x 24" rectangular ruler and a 12" square ruler are good for cutting strips and background squares and squaring up blocks. I also use a smaller 6" square ruler called a Bias Square®. It is ruled with ⅛" markings and is very handy to keep by your sewing machine for taking measurements while you work. There are several brands of rotary cutting mats available. I prefer an 18" x 24" self-healing type for cutting strips and squares. A smaller mat is better for working with scraps or for keeping by your sewing machine. Most of these items are available at quilt shops or fabric shops.

Thread

Use good-quality thread for all your piecing and quilting. It is always a challenge to select a thread color when working with contrasting fabric colors. A neutral color, such as light gray or ecru, works well for most color combinations, and 100 percent–cotton or cotton-covered polyester thread is best for piecing. For machine quilting, use 100 percent cotton or cotton-covered polyester, but never use nylon. Embroidery thread works well in place of nylon, as it is similar in weight. Use 100 percent–cotton or cotton-covered polyester quilting thread for hand quilting.

Needles

For machine piecing, a size 10/70 or 12/80 needle works well for most cottons. For hand sewing and appliqué, use #11 or #12 Sharps, which are thinner than other sewing needles. For hand quilting, use #8, #9, or #10 Betweens. Betweens are shorter and thinner than regular sewing needles, allowing you to work through the layers of a quilt more easily and make smaller stitches. The rule of thumb with needles is that the larger the number of the needle, the smaller the needle is. Make sure to start any project with a new, sharp needle. A dull needle can cause skipped stitches and distort your fabric.

Pins

For piecing blocks, I use silk pins, which have a very fine shank that glides easily in and out of the fabric. If you are working with multiple layers, the longer quilting pins with plastic heads are easy to handle. Small ½" to ¾" long sequin pins work well for appliqué. For basting a project that will be machine quilted, use 1"-long, rust-proof, nickel-plated safety pins.

Scissors

Good scissors will last a lifetime. Use your best scissors for cutting fabric only. Make sure the family knows that your sewing scissors are not for general use. If you need to, hide them. Use an older pair of scissors to cut paper, cardboard, and template plastic. Keep a pair of small, 4" scissors with sharp points next to your sewing machine for clipping threads.

Template Plastic

Making templates is a very important step when working on a quilt. Use clear or frosted plastic (available at quilt shops) to make durable, accurate templates. Trace the patterns onto the template plastic with a permanent, fine-point marker.

Seam Ripper

Use this "reverse sewing" tool to remove stitches from incorrectly sewn seams. A seam ripper can also be used in place of a stiletto, to help guide fabrics through the sewing machine or hold seam intersections together while piecing.

Marking Tools

Use a sharp No. 2 pencil or fine-lead mechanical pencil for marking on lighter fabrics, and a silver or yellow marking pencil on darker fabrics. Chalk pencils or chalk-wheel markers also make clear marks on fabric. Be sure to test any marking tool to make sure you can remove the marks easily. Never use an ink pen or permanent marker to mark quilting designs on fabric.

Sewing Machine

Any machine that sews a good straight stitch is fine. But it is important to be familiar with the machine you are using. Practice sewing on scraps until you are comfortable, or remove the thread from the machine and practice on paper. If you do practice on paper, remember to change the needle before actually piecing your project. Sewing on paper dulls your needle, and you should use a sharp needle when sewing on fabric.

You will also need a walking foot or darning foot if you are going to machine quilt. Make sure the tension is adjusted and your stitches are even. Use a new needle that will glide smoothly in and out of the fabric. A dull needle can snag fabric or distort seams.

Before sewing, clean all surfaces of your sewing machine with an absorbent cloth. This will ensure that oil and dirt will not get on the blocks or quilt as you work.

Iron and Ironing Board

For accurate piecing, careful pressing is a must. Keep your iron and ironing board as close to your sewing area as possible. You may spray fabrics with water or fabric sizing when pressing, but it is best not to use steam. Steam can stretch fabric and make it difficult to work with, especially when you are working with bias edges. If you prefer to work with steam, be very careful, and remember to let the iron glide over the surface of the fabric.

Rotary Cutting

Instructions for quick and easy rotary cutting are provided wherever possible. All measurements include standard ¼"-wide seam allowances. Before rotary cutting any fabric, refer to "Content, Care, and Style" on page 9 to wash, dry, and press all fabrics to be used in any of the projects in this book. For those unfamiliar with rotary cutting, brief guidelines are provided here. For more detailed information, see Donna Lynn Thomas's *Shortcuts: A Concise Guide to Rotary Cutting* (That Patchwork Place, 1999). It is important to observe these simple safety rules any time you use a rotary cutter:

- Remember to close the safety shield every time the rotary cutter is not in use.
- Always roll the rotary cutter away from you, never toward you or under your other hand or arm.
- Hold the rotary cutting ruler firmly in place as you cut. Keep your fingers away from the edge of the ruler.
- Follow the manufacturer's instructions for safe disposal of old rotary cutting blades.
- Keep your rotary cutter stored in a safe place that is out of the reach of children.

Strips

To rotary cut squares, rectangles, and triangles, you will first need to cut straight strips of fabric. The following steps will help you cut accurately and quickly, with little waste of fabric.

1. Fold the fabric and match the selvages, aligning the crosswise and lengthwise grains as much as possible. Place the folded edge closest to you on the cutting mat. For all rotary cutting, the fabric should be placed to your right (reverse if you are left-handed). Align a square acrylic ruler along the folded edge of the fabric. Then place a long, straight ruler to the left of the square ruler, just covering the uneven, raw edges of the left side of the fabric.

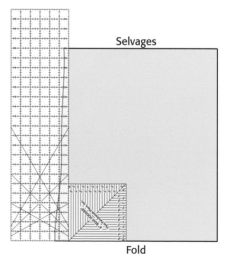

Selvages

Fold

2. Remove the square ruler and cut along the right edge of the long ruler. Hold the ruler down with your left hand as you cut, pressing firmly and keeping your fingers away from the ruler's edge. Roll the rotary cutter away from you. Discard the narrow strip of fabric. Reverse this procedure if you are left-handed.

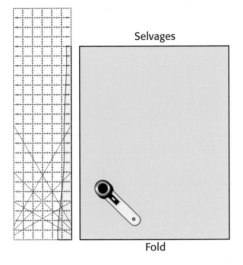

3. To rotary cut strips, fold the fabric in half again, aligning the fold with the selvages. Align the required strip width measurement on the long ruler with the newly straightened left edge of the fabric. For example, to cut a 3"-wide strip, place the 3" ruler mark on the edge of the fabric.

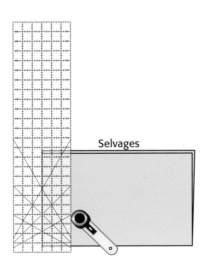

Squares

To rotary cut squares, start by cutting a strip that is the measurement of the finished square, plus seam allowances. Trim away the selvage ends of the strip. Align the required square measurement on the ruler with the left edge of the strip and cut the number of squares needed.

Rectangles

Rotary cut rectangles in the same manner as squares. First, use the shorter measurement of the rectangle, including seam allowances, to cut a strip; then use the longer measurement, which should also include seam allowances, to cut the strip into the number of rectangles needed. Because none of the projects in this book call for half-square triangles or quarter-square triangles, those instructions are not included.

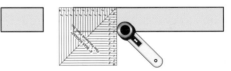

Machine Piecing

Seam Allowances

The most important thing to remember about machine piecing is to maintain a consistent ¼"-wide seam allowance. Otherwise, the quilt blocks will not be the desired finished size. If that happens, the size of everything else in the quilt will be affected, including alternate blocks, sashings, and borders. The measurements for all components of each quilt are based on blocks that finish accurately to the desired size, plus ¼" on each edge for seam allowances.

Take the time to establish an exact ¼"-wide seam guide on your machine. Some machines have a special quilting foot that measures exactly ¼" from the center needle position to the edge of the foot. If your machine doesn't have this type of foot, create a seam guide by placing the edge of a piece of tape, moleskin, or a magnetic seam guide exactly ¼" to the right of the needle.

Strip Piecing

Strip piecing is a quick, easy, and accurate way to make several units that are repeated in a pattern. It significantly speeds up the quiltmaking process and improves accuracy. When strip piecing, first cut strips on the crosswise grain of the fabric. To determine the width to cut strips, add a ¼" seam allowance to each side of the finished dimension of the shape you need. For example, if the finished dimension of a square is to be 3", cut a 3½"-wide strip. Strip widths for all projects include ¼"-wide seam allowances on all sides. For an example of strip piecing, refer to the following section, "Four-Patch Units."

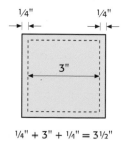

¼" + 3" + ¼" = 3½"

The following steps describe the process for making a four-patch unit.

1. Sew a light and a dark strip of fabric together with ¼" seams.
2. Press the seam allowances toward the darker fabric. Press from the right side of the fabric as well to avoid pleating along the seam lines.
3. From the strip set, cut segments in the width required for your project.

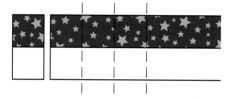

4. Stitch segments together, alternating colors. Use a ¼"-wide seam allowance to form each four-patch unit. Press the seam allowances to one side.

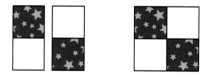

Pressing

The traditional rule in quiltmaking is to press seam allowances to one side, toward the darker color wherever possible. First, press the seam from the wrong side; then press it in the desired direction from the right side. Press carefully, to avoid distorting the pieced shapes. Remember to let the iron glide over the surface of the fabric.

When joining two seamed units together, press the seam allowances in opposite directions to reduce bulk. Where the two units meet, the seam allowances will butt against each other, making it easier to join the seam intersections perfectly.

14

Appliqué

All of the projects in this book were made with fusible appliqué and the buttonhole stitch, but they could also be made with regular hand appliqué. Instructions are provided for both hand and fusible appliqué. Choose one of the following methods, or use your own favorite appliqué technique.

Making Templates

For appliqué, I prefer to make templates from clear plastic rather than other materials such as cardboard. Clear plastic templates are more durable, and you can see through the plastic, which makes it is easy to see the fabrics as you trace. To make the templates, place template plastic over each pattern piece, and trace the shape with a fine-tip permanent marker. Do not add seam allowances when making templates for appliqué. Cut out the templates on the drawn lines. You will need only one template for each different shape. Mark the pattern name and grain-line arrow (if applicable) on the template.

Hand Appliqué

The following steps describe the hand-appliqué process:

1. To begin to hand appliqué, first place the template right side up on the right side of the appliqué fabric. Trace around the template. Leave at least ½" between tracings, if you will be marking several pieces on the same piece of fabric. Cut out each appliqué shape. Add a scant ¼" seam allowance around the traced line. This seam allowance will be turned under to create the finished edge of the appliqué. On very small pieces, you may wish to add only ⅛" seam allowances for easier handling. Turn

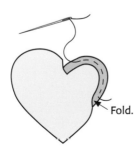

Fold.

under the seam allowance of each appliqué by using the pencil line as a guide, and finger press it. Baste close to the turned edge to hold the seam allowance in place. Clip where needed.

2. After the appliqué pieces are basted, pin the pieces in place on the background fabric. Note where one piece is overlapped by another. When one appliqué piece is covered or overlapped by another, you will want to stitch the underneath piece to the background fabric first. The rule with hand appliqué blocks is to always work from the background to the foreground. Leave any edge that will be overlapped by another piece unstitched. Dotted lines on the pattern indicate areas of overlap.

3. To stitch the appliqué pieces to the quilt top by hand, thread a #11 or #12 Sharps or Milliner's needle with a single strand of thread that is approximately 18" long. Tie a knot in the end.

Note: Match the thread color to the appliqué fabric, not to the background fabric. Lightweight, 100 percent–cotton machine embroidery thread works well for hand appliqué.

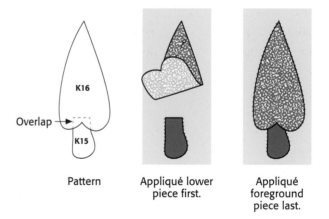

Pattern   Appliqué lower   Appliqué
                piece first.   foreground
                                      piece last.

4. Hide the knot by slipping the needle into the seam allowance from the wrong side of the appliqué piece and bring it out on the fold line.

5. Start the first stitch by moving the needle straight off the appliqué and inserting it into the background fabric. Let the needle travel underneath the background fabric, parallel to the edge of the appliqué, and bring it up about ⅛" away. On the right side of your work, the

stitches will look small and straight, and on the back side of your work, they will appear small and slightly slanted. Work from right to left if you are right-handed and left to right if you are left-handed.

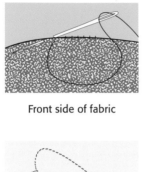

Front side of fabric

Back side of fabric

6. As you bring the needle up, pierce the folded edge of the appliqué piece. Catch only one or two threads of the edge. Pull the thread through and give the thread a slight tug.

7. Move the needle straight off the appliqué piece and insert it into the background fabric again. Let the needle travel under the background fabric, bring it up about ⅛" away, and catch the folded edge of the appliqué piece. Give the thread a slight tug and continue stitching.

8. To end a line of stitching, pull the needle through to the wrong side. Behind the appliqué piece, take 2 small stitches and make knots by taking your needle through the loops. Check the right side of your work to see if the thread shows through the background fabric. If it does, take one more small stitch on the back side to direct the tail of the thread under the appliqué fabric. Remove the basting stitches that were holding the seam allowances in place.

Outer Points

As you stitch toward an outer point, start taking smaller stitches within ½" of the point. Trim the seam allowance or use the tip of your needle to push the excess fabric underneath the point. The smaller stitches near the point will keep any frayed edges from escaping. Place the last stitch on the first side of the appliqué piece very close to the point. Place the next stitch on the adjacent side of the point. A stitch on each side, very close to the point, will accent the outer point.

Inner Points

Make your stitches smaller when you reach an area within ½" of an inner point. If your inner points fray, do a few very close stitches to tack the fabric down securely. If your thread matches your appliqué fabric exactly, these stitches will blend in with the edge of the shape.

Inner Curves

Make clips in the seam allowances of concave or inner curves, if necessary, to allow you to turn them under easily. Push the fabric under with the tip of your needle, smoothing it out along the folded edge before stitching it in place.

Fusible Appliqué

Fusible appliqué is a quick method that requires some type of stitching around the fused pieces. Because fusible web can add thickness to your appliqué, choose a lightweight fusible web for your projects. Always follow the manufacturer's directions for the fusible web product you select. The patterns for the projects in this book are drawn so that you will need to *reverse* them when you use fusible web. If you have not made templates, trace the full pattern onto tracing paper. Turn the tracing-paper pattern face down. Place the fusible web, paper side up, over the pattern. Retrace the pattern pieces individually onto the paper side of the fusible web. Do not add seam allowances to the appliqué pieces when you cut them for fusible appliqué. Position and fuse the appliqué pieces in order on the background fabric so that the pieces overlap as shown in the quilt photos and quilt diagrams.

To make the placement of fusible appliqués easier, I like to use The Appliqué Pressing Sheet. Place the transparent pressing sheet over the project pattern and layer the appliqué shapes onto the pressing sheet instead of the fabric. Press each piece as you go. With this product, you can fuse your design together into one unit before you press it onto the background fabric. Your appliqué unit will peel right off the pressing sheet. This sheet also eliminates the problem of small pieces shifting.

After the appliqué pieces are fused in place on the background block, outline each piece with embroidery stitches, as indicated in the pattern. There are several different stitches used for the projects in this book. Refer to "Embellishments," which follows this section, for instructions on how to make these stitches.

Embellishments

Embellishing a block is a way to add finishing touches and dimension and turn something average into something magical. Embellishments can be functional, such as the buttonhole stitch, or decorative, like buttons. The most common form of embellishment is embroidery, which adds color, dimension, and texture. All of the fusible appliqué projects in this book use either the buttonhole stitch or the running stitch to secure each piece. Some of the other stitches that can be used for the snowman projects are the stem or outline stitch, the backstitch, the cross-stitch, and the satin stitch.

Buttonhole Stitch

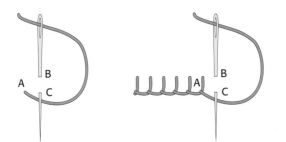

The buttonhole stitch defines appliqué shapes and adds dimension to a project. It is a common stitch that has a variety of applications, both practical and decorative. It is frequently used for finishing raw edges. You can make it look more decorative by altering the lengths of the vertical straight stitches. A simple variation is to make the vertical stitches

alternately long and short, either alone or in groups of two or three.

The buttonhole stitch is worked from left to right. To begin, use a sharp embroidery needle and two or three strands of embroidery floss 18"–20" long. You may also do buttonhole stitching with pearl cotton thread. Use one strand of number 8 pearl cotton thread. This will give a thicker edging to your project. Thread the needle and make a knot at the end of the thread. Referring to the diagram, pull the needle up at A. Form a right angle shape with the floss. Hold the angled loop in place with your finger and insert the needle back through the fabric at B. Slide it through to C, with the point of the needle over the thread. Pull the thread through and repeat this process for each stitch. The line that connects the stitches should lie against the cut edge of the appliqué piece. Make sure that the vertical stitches are straight and even.

To end a line of buttonhole stitching, insert the needle in the back side of your work and weave a small amount of thread into previous stitches to secure the end of the floss. Clip the end of the floss close to the surface of your stitching. Buttonhole stitch around the appliqué pieces in each block before assembling the blocks into rows.

Running Stitch

The running stitch is the simplest and most basic of all embroidery stitches. It is made simply by passing the needle and thread in and out of the fabric at regular intervals, much like a hand-basting stitch. To start or end the stitch, make a regular sewing knot on the back side of the quilt. You can use the running stitch as an outline stitch or for the primitive look of stitching in the ditch, which is explained in the section "Machine Quilting" on pages 23–24. You can use any type of embroidery thread to do running stitches as long as the thread you choose is compatible with the weight of the fabric.

Stem Stitch

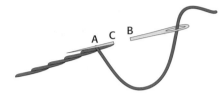

The stem stitch is one of the most frequently used outline stitches. It is quite easy to work and follows curves very well. This stitch is worked with a forward and a backward motion. The stitches should be even and equal in size. If you are going for a more primitive look, you can make your stitches slightly irregular. *Note: If you keep the working thread to the right of the needle, the effect will be slightly different and the resulting stitch is known as the outline stitch.*

Backstitch

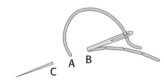

Backstitching is one of the most adaptable of all hand embroidery stitches. It can be worked in small, even stitches for delicate work (which looks rather like machine stitching) or in larger, less even stitches for a more primitive look. This stitch follows curves well if the stitches are kept small. Bring the needle up at A, take a small stitch backward and go down at B, and slide the needle to come out at C. Keep the distance between A and B equal.

Cross-Stitch

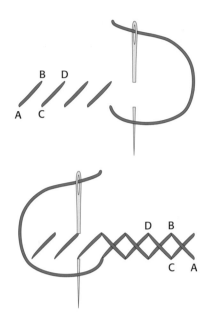

The cross-stitch is probably the oldest and best known of all decorative embroidery stitches. It is extremely quick and easy to work. It is used in the quilts for eyes, snowman buttons, and lettering. Referring to the diagrams below, bring the needle up at A. Take the needle up and across an equal distance to B, go down at B, then come up at C. Go down at D and continue, stitching the number of required stitches to form a row of half Xs. Work back in the opposite direction, repeating the steps to complete the Xs. Cross-stitching may be worked from right to left or left to right, whichever you prefer. All top stitches should slant in the same direction.

Satin Stitch

This stitch is used to fill areas such as noses on your snowman. It covers an area completely.

Adding Ribbon

We are lucky to have so many different types of ribbon, rickrack, braid, lace and other trims available today, in widths from 1.5 mm to 90 mm. These types of trim can be topstitched onto appliqué. You can use the narrowest satin ribbon to form branches and stems. Not only do they give appliqué extra dimension, but they also add personality and charm.

Using Markers

Markers are an easy way to add detail to appliqué. Faces, lettering, and even faux quilting lines can be added to blocks with markers. There is a wide range of markers now available, but before drawing any design, consider which variety of marker will best suit your needs. Always test markers on a scrap of fabric before using them on the fabric for your project. I used a fine-tip fabric marker for the projects in this book. Once you decide which marker to use, cut out an appliqué piece and place it over the pattern to trace details directly onto the fabric. If your fabric is a light color, the pattern lines will be easily visible to trace. However, if you are using dark fabric, you may need to place the fabric and pattern over a light source such as a light table or window.

Buttons and Beads

Readily available at most quilt and craft stores, buttons and beads come in a wide variety of shapes, sizes, colors, and finishes. They are an inexpensive way to add sparkle, color, and a touch of whimsy to a project. Small beads or buttons can add a lot of fun with little time and trouble. Add them last because of their weight. And don't feel that you have to use the same embellishments shown in the projects in this book. Choose the ones that you like the most, and add your own ideas to make your project unique.

Embroidery Floss

Embroidery floss is the most popular of all decorative threads used for embellishing. Floss comes in an extensive range of colors, both plain and variegated forms. And although most types of floss are colorfast, it is a good idea to test for colorfastness if you are planning to wash the project you are making. Floss is composed of six strands and can be used whole or separated into the number of stands called for in a particular pattern. If your pattern calls for separating the thread, remember to cut the length you need before separating the threads for easier handling.

Pearl Cotton

Pearl cotton is a pure cotton, two-ply thread that is twisted together to produce a beaded effect. It is available in several weights: the larger the number, the finer the thread weight. Pearl cotton has a good sheen, comes in a wide range of colors, and is often substituted for embroidery floss. You can use it for any of the projects in this book that call for embroidery floss.

Finishing a Quilt

Several steps are required to finish a quilt, including squaring-up blocks; adding borders; choosing and marking quilting designs; layering the top, batting, and backing; quilting; and binding. As you begin this process, examine the wrong side of the quilt top closely. Try to trim all loose threads and make sure your top is flat with square sides.

Squaring-Up Blocks

Sometimes blocks can get distorted because of the type of fabric you choose or the pressing method you use. Use a clear, acrylic ruler to measure your finished blocks, and if necessary, trim them to the correct size.

Borders

Borders frame a quilt, just like a mat and frame around a picture or painting. For best results, do not cut border strips and sew them directly to the quilt sides without measuring first. The edges of a quilt often measure slightly longer than the distance measured through the quilt center because of stretching during construction. Measure the quilt top through the center in both directions to determine how long to cut the border strips. You can then ease the quilt edges into the cut borders, if necessary. This step ensures that the finished quilt will be as straight and as square as possible, without wavy edges.

To make borders, follow these steps:

1. Measure the length of the quilt top from top to bottom, through the center. Cut 2 border strips to that measurement, piecing as necessary. Mark the center of the side edges on the quilt top, and the center of the 2 border strips with a pin. Pin the borders to the sides of the quilt top, matching the centers and ends, and easing as necessary. Sew the border strips in place. Press the seams toward the border strips.

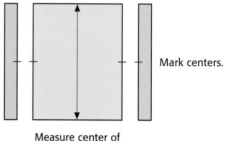

Mark centers.

Measure center of
quilt, top to bottom.

2. Measure the width of the quilt top from side to side, through the center, including the side borders you just attached. Cut 2 border strips to that measurement, piecing as necessary. Use a pin to mark the center of the top and bottom edges of the quilt top and the center of the border strips. Pin the borders to the top and bottom edges of the quilt top, matching the centers and ends and easing, as necessary. Sew the border strips to the quilt top. Press the seams toward the borders.

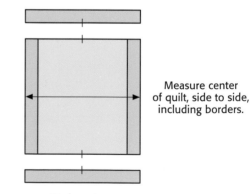

Measure center
of quilt, side to side,
including borders.

Mark centers.

Marking Quilting Lines

Whether or not to mark quilting designs depends upon the type of quilting you want to do. Marking is not necessary if you plan to quilt in the ditch or outline quilt a uniform distance from seam lines. These quilting techniques are described in "Machine Quilting" on pages 23–24. For more complex quilting designs, however, mark the design on the quilt top before layering it with the batting and backing. You can create your own quilting design or buy quilting stencils made from durable plastic at a quilt shop.

Choose a marking tool that will be visible on your fabric. Experiment with different types of marking tools to decide which one you like best before marking a large area of your quilt. Test the tool on fabric scraps to be sure that you can remove the marks easily. You can also use masking tape to mark straight quilting lines. Tape only small sections at a time, and remove the tape when you stop at the end of the day; otherwise, the sticky residue may be difficult to remove from the fabric.

Some continuous, free-motion quilting designs may also need to be marked so that they are easier to stitch. If you choose a design like this, wait until you are ready to quilt an area before marking the design, and only mark a small area at a time. This type of quilting can sometimes rub the marked lines off of the quilt top.

Backing and Batting

The quilt "sandwich" consists of a layer of backing fabric, batting, and the quilt top itself. Cut the quilt backing at least 2" larger than the quilt top all the way around. For large quilts, it is usually necessary to sew two or three lengths of fabric together to make a large enough backing. Trim away the selvages before piecing the lengths of fabric together. Press the seams in the backing open to make quilting easier. Some fabrics are available in 90" or 108" widths. Using one of these wider fabrics will usually eliminate the need to piece the backing for your quilt.

Batting comes packaged in standard bed sizes or on large rolls, which allows you to purchase it by the yard. Several weights, or thicknesses, are available today. Thick battings are fine for tied quilts and comforters. A thinner batting is better, however, if you intend to quilt by hand or machine. Whatever batting you choose, take it out of the bag and let it relax for a day or two before you use it. Also check the manufacturer's recommendations for the closeness of quilting required for that particular batting. This will influence how closely you decide to quilt. Just like the backing, the batting should be 2" larger than the quilt top on all sides.

Layering and Basting

Whether you intend to quilt by hand or machine, a well-basted quilt makes the quilting process easier. The following steps describe how to layer and baste your quilt.

1. Spread the backing, wrong side up, on a flat, clean surface. Anchor it with pins or masking tape. Be careful not to stretch the backing out of shape.
2. Spread the batting evenly over the backing, smoothing out any wrinkles.
3. Center the pressed quilt top on top of the batting, right side up. Smooth out any wrinkles and make sure that the edges of the quilt top are parallel to the edges of the backing.

4. Starting in the center and working diagonally toward each corner, baste the 3 layers together by hand. Continue basting a grid of horizontal and vertical lines. Space them 6" to 8" apart. Finish by basting around the edges.

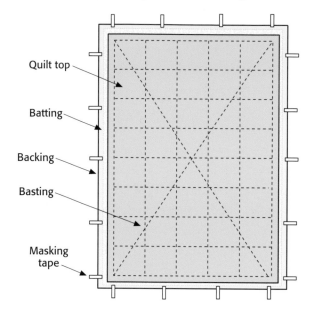

Quilt top

Batting

Backing

Basting

Masking tape

5. For machine quilting, you may baste the layers with 1" long, rustproof, nickel-plated safety pins. Begin pin-basting in the center of the quilt, and work toward the edges. Place the pins about 6" to 8" apart and stay away from areas where you intend to quilt.

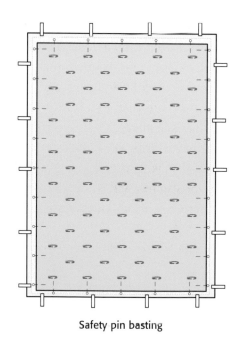

Safety pin basting

Hand Quilting

To quilt by hand, you will need short, sturdy needles called Betweens, quilting thread, and a thimble to fit the middle finger of your sewing hand. Most quilters also use a frame or hoop to support their work. Use the smallest needle you can comfortably handle; the finer the needle, the smaller your quilting stitches will be.

The following steps describe how to hand quilt.

1. Secure the area to be quilted in a hoop. Check the quilt top and backing to make sure they are smooth, with no wrinkles or puckered areas.

2. Thread a needle with a single strand of quilting thread that is about 18" long. Make a small knot in the thread, and insert the needle into the top layer of the quilt sandwich, about 1" from the place where you want to start stitching. Pull the needle out at the point where quilting will begin and gently pull the thread until the knot pops through the fabric and into the batting layer.

3. Take small, evenly spaced running stitches through all 3 layers of the quilt sandwich. The quilting stitch forms a broken line on both the quilt top and the backing. Rock the needle up and down through all 3 layers until you have 3 or 4 stitches on the needle, and then pull the needle through. When stitching, place your other hand underneath the layered quilt sandwich so that you can feel the needle point with the tip of your finger each time it comes through the backing fabric.

4. To end a line of hand quilting stitches, make a small knot close to the last stitch. Then backstitch, running the thread a needle's length through the batting. Gently pull the thread until the knot pops into the batting, and clip the thread at the quilt's surface. For more information on hand quilting, refer to the book *Loving Stitches: A Guide to Fine Hand Quilting,* by Jeana Kimball (That Patchwork Place, 1992).

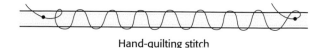

Hand-quilting stitch

Machine Quilting

Machine quilting is suitable for all sizes and types of quilts, from crib to full-size bed quilts. Machine quilting allows you to quickly complete quilts that might otherwise languish on the shelves. Marking the quilting lines is only necessary if you need to follow a grid or a complex pattern. It is not necessary for quilting in the ditch, outline quilting a uniform distance from seam lines, or free-motion quilting random patterns. For machine quilting, you will need the following tools and supplies:

- Sewing machine in good working condition
- Walking foot attachment (on some machines, this is built in) for quilting straight lines like cross-hatching or quilting in the ditch
- Darning foot for free-motion quilting or stippling

Quilting in the Ditch

The seam lines that join sashing strips and borders are referred to as "ditches." To quilt in the ditch by machine, follow these steps.

1. Attach a walking (even-feed) foot to your sewing machine. This foot will allow the layers of the quilt sandwich to feed through the sewing machine evenly.

Walking foot attachment

2. Position the quilt sandwich under the sewing machine needle, at the place where you want to start quilting. Take 1 stitch and pull up the bobbin thread so that both the top and bobbin threads are on top of the quilt. This will prevent a tangled mess from forming on the backing of your quilt. Take 2 or 3 stitches in place at your starting spot to secure the threads, and begin stitching.

3. Gently spread the fabrics apart as you quilt in the ditch of the seam line, and try to maintain an even pace as you stitch. Plan your stitching course before you begin so that there will be as few starts and stops as possible. Do not watch the needle, but rather, focus an inch or two ahead of where you are actually stitching.

4. When you reach a stopping point, secure the line of quilting by taking 2 or 3 stitches in place. Clip the thread close to the surface of the quilt.

Free-Motion Quilting

Free-motion quilting takes a lot of practice, but the more you do, the easier it gets. Practice on a little quilt or on a few blocks before tackling a bigger project. Follow these steps to do beautiful free-motion machine quilting.

1. Attach a darning foot to your sewing machine.

Darning foot

2. Disengage the feed dogs on your machine.
3. Pull the bobbin thread up to the top of the quilt so that it doesn't get tangled underneath. Stitch randomly, or follow continuous free-motion quilting designs that do not require lots of stopping and starting. Guide the quilt under the needle with both hands. Move it at an even pace so that your quilting lines will be smooth and your stitches will be even in length.
4. If you have open areas, try stipple quilting as a filler. Stipple quilting works well with most block patterns and background areas of

appliqué designs, and does not detract from the overall design of the quilt. As you stitch, take care to keep your stitching lines separated; do not cross a previous line of stipple quilting.

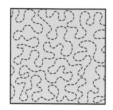

5. To end a line of free-motion quilting, set the stitch length on your machine to 0 and take a few stitches. Clip the thread on the top and bottom of the quilt.

Binding

The binding finishes the raw edges of a quilt. You can cut binding strips from the straight grain or bias of the fabric. All of the projects in this book feature straight-grain binding, which is faster and easier to cut than bias binding. However, bias binding is a must for quilts with curves, and it is well worth the extra effort. The following steps describe how to make and apply binding to the quilt.

1. When the quilting is complete, trim away the excess batting and backing on all sides of the quilt. Remove any remaining basting threads or pins. Choose the fabric you want to use for binding the quilt.

2. To make straight-grain binding, cut 2½"-wide strips across the 42" width of the fabric. You will need enough strips to go around the perimeter of the quilt, plus 10" extra to allow for the seams and the mitered corner folds. Sew the short ends of the cut binding strips right sides together to make one long binding piece.

3. Trim one end of the strip at a 45° angle. Turn under ¼" and press the fold.

4. Fold the binding in half lengthwise, wrong sides together, and press the entire binding strip.

Fold line

5. Starting away from a corner on one side of the quilt, use a ¼"-wide seam allowance and stitch the binding to the quilt. Keep the raw edges of the binding even with the edge of the quilt top. Stop stitching ¼" from the corner of the quilt top, and backstitch. Clip the thread.

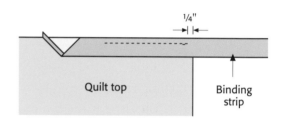

1/4"

Quilt top

Binding strip

6. Turn the quilt so that you will be stitching down the next side. Fold the binding up, away from the quilt as shown in the diagram. Fold the binding back down on top of itself so that it is even with the edge of the quilt top. Begin stitching ¼" from the edge. Backstitch to secure the beginning of this seam.

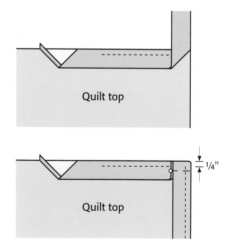

Quilt top

1/4"

Quilt top

7. Repeat this process for the remaining sides and corners of the quilt. When you reach your starting point, trim the end of the binding at a 45° angle. Make sure that you leave enough to tuck inside the beginning of the binding, usually about 1". Tuck the end of the binding into the fold at the beginning of the binding, and finish stitching the binding seam.

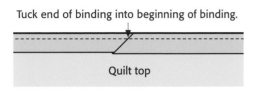

Tuck end of binding into beginning of binding.

Quilt top

8. Fold the binding over to the back side of the quilt, with the folded edge covering the row of machine stitching and a 45°-angle fold forming at the corner. Blindstitch the binding in place by hand. At each corner, bring the fold in and a mitered fold will form. Blindstitch the mitered corner folds in place.

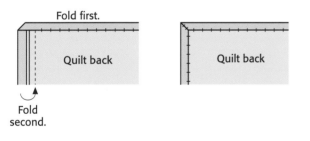

Fold first.

Quilt back

Quilt back

Fold second.

Sleeves

If you plan to display your quilt on a wall, you will need to add a hanging sleeve near the top edge of the backing to hold a hanging rod. To make a 4"-wide sleeve, follow these steps.

1. Cut a strip of backing fabric (or muslin) that is 8½" wide and 3" shorter than the width of the quilt.

2. Turn under ½" on each of the short ends and press. Turn under another ½", and stitch a hem at the ends of the sleeve.

3. Fold the strip of fabric in half lengthwise, wrong sides together, and press. Stitch a ¼" seam along the length of the raw edges to form a tube.

4. Fold the tube so that the seam is centered on one side, and press the seam allowances open.

5. Place the sleeve against the backing of the quilt, with the seam allowances lying next to the quilt.

6. Position the top folded edge of the sleeve so that it touches the bottom edge of the binding. Pin the sleeve in place.

7. Hand stitch the top and bottom folds of the sleeve to the backing fabric. Be careful not to go through to the front side of the quilt as you stitch.

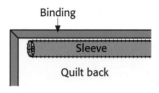

Binding

Sleeve

Quilt back

Note: For smaller quilts or wall hangings, the sleeve seam can be basted to the top raw edge of the quilt and sewn under the binding. This will eliminate hand stitching the top edge of the sleeve on the backing fabric.

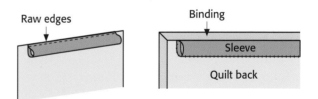

Raw edges

Binding

Sleeve

Quilt back

Signing a Quilt

Be sure to make a quilt label for your quilt. This is a very important step in the quiltmaking process. Keep in mind that future generations will be interested in learning more than just who made the quilt, and when. Some suggestions for what to include are the name of the quilt, your own name, the names of the city and state where you live, the date when you finished the quilt, and the name of the recipient (if it is a gift). The information you feature can be handwritten, typed, or embroidered. Follow the steps below to make and appliqué the label to the back of the quilt.

1. Cut a square of fabric that will accommodate the amount of information you want to put on the label.

2. Center a piece of freezer paper, with the shiny side down, on the wrong side of the fabric. Iron the freezer paper to the fabric. This will stabilize the fabric label for writing.

3. Hand write the information on the right side of the fabric with a fine-point, permanent marking pen. Leave a ¼" margin around all edges.

4. After you finish writing, remove the freezer paper from the fabric.

5. If you want to embroider your label, pick an embroidery floss color to match the pen color. Use your favorite embroidery stitch to embroider the letters. Then press under the ¼" margins as seam allowances, and position the label on the back of the quilt. Baste the label in place by hand.

6. Appliqué the label to the backing of the quilt. Be very careful to stitch the label only to the backing fabric.

A Snowman's Family Album

A Snowman's Family Album *by Mary M. Covey, 1999, Jenks, Oklahoma, 62" x 62".*

The Snowman Blocks

As an avid photographer, I loved collecting pictures, much in the same way that I now enjoy collecting fabric. After developing each roll of film, I would put the photos into a shoebox labeled with things like "baseball games," "birthday parties," or "school plays." When I was ready to put the photos in albums, it was easy to grab the right shoebox and begin filling the pages. For making "A Snowman's Family Album" quilt, I encourage you to try this same system. Purchase two boxes, one for fabrics and one for embellishments. I buy clear or opaque plastic boxes at a thrift store for under $2 each. Take some time to go through your fabric stash and pull out every fabric you think will work in your quilt. Place the fabrics in a box and label it with a piece of tape that has the project name on it. In addition to the fabric, store everything you think you might need, such as batting and the quilt pattern, in the box as well. Place embellishments such as buttons, embroidery floss, small pieces of trim, and jingle bells in the other box.

When you go to a quilt shop or fabric store, take your "A Snowman's Family Album" quilt box with you to help coordinate the fabrics for your quilt. Storing the materials for your projects in this way is a time saver that will help you avoid spending hours looking for that perfect piece of fabric you saw three months ago but cannot find now. It will also make sure that you do not use fabric you bought specifically for this project in another quilt.

After you finish the project, you can remove the tape label from the box, place any leftover fabrics back in your stash, and use the same box for your next project. I like to keep a number of marked project boxes in my closet, ready to pull out at a moment's notice. That way, even if I only have a few minutes for sewing, everything I need is in one place and easy to find. If I piece only one block or buttonhole stitch around just a few shapes, I am that much further ahead.

Because each block in "A Snowman's Family Album" quilt is different in size and design, the best way to construct this quilt is to make one block at a time. The cutting and assembly instructions for each individual block, along with A filler strips and B filler strips, are presented with each block. After constructing all of the blocks and filler strips for your quilt, follow the assembly instructions for putting everything together to make the finished quilt top.

Materials
42"-wide fabric

½ yd. each of red, green, yellow, and blue fabrics for filler strips

2 yds. (total) assorted white-on-white prints for filler strips, backgrounds, and appliqué pieces

2½ yds. (total) assorted blue fabrics for backgrounds; include several lights, mediums, and darks in a variety of designs

¼ yd. light blue fabric for Four Patch filler blocks

⅛ yd. tan fabric for sand

⅛ yd. green fabric for grass

⅛ yd. brown fabric for ground

⅛ yd. red-and-white stripe for candy canes and appliqué pieces

Assorted large scraps of colorful fabrics for appliqué pieces

⅓ yd. yellow fabric for inner border

⅝ yd. each of red fabric and white fabric for checkerboard border

4 yds. fabric for backing and hanging sleeve

66" x 66" piece of batting

¾ yd. red fabric for binding

4 yds. fusible web

Assorted colors of embroidery floss to match appliqué pieces

Buttons, beads, fleece, ribbon, and rickrack for embellishing

Permanent fabric marker

A Filler Strips

As you construct the blocks for your snowman quilt, sew these A filler strips end to end until they reach the necessary length. Add the strips according to the block instructions to the top, bottom, or side of a block. Trim the strips even with the edges of the block.

1. To make A filler strips, cut a 1½" x 42" strip from each of the red, green, yellow, blue, and white fabrics for filler strips.

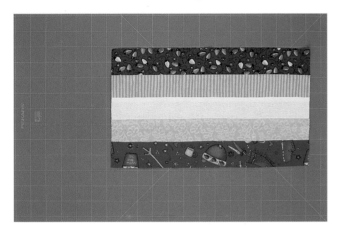

2. Referring to the photo, sew the strips together to form a unit. Press the seams in one direction—all to the right or all to the left.
3. Cut the unit into 2"-wide strips.

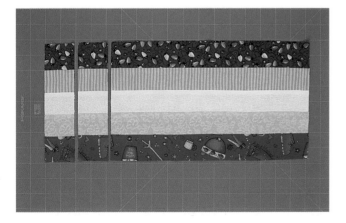

D Filler Strips

As you construct the various blocks, sew these B filler strips end to end until they reach the necessary length. Add the strips according to the block instructions to the top, bottom, or side of a block. Trim the strips even with the edges of the block.

1. To make B filler strips, cut a 2½" x 42" strip from each of the red, yellow, blue, white, and green fabrics for filler strips.
2. Referring to the photo, sew the strips together to form a unit. Press the seams in one direction—all to the right or all to the left.

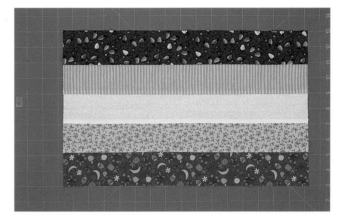

3. Cut the unit into 2 ½"-wide strips.

Quilt Plan

block I

A Snowman at Birth

Finished Size: 12" x 12"

No family album would be complete without pictures of each new arrival. What proud parents would not be overjoyed to send out pictures of their new child? This is the picture that appears in this snowman's birth announcement, showing his weight as 6 snowflakes, 2 ice crystals. Even at just a few snowflakes old, it was clear that this was going to be no ordinary snowman.

Directions

1. From a blue background fabric, cut one 12½" square.
2. From a white-on-white print, cut one 10" square.
3. From the fusible web, cut a 9" square. Iron the fusible web to the wrong side of the white 10" square. Allow ½" of fabric to remain free on all 4 sides of the fabric square.

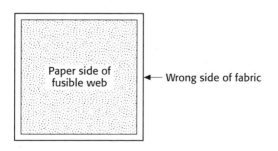

4. Trim away the ½" of fabric around all sides of the white square.

5. With the fusible web paper still attached, refer to the diagram to cut the 9" square from step 3 into six 3" squares and two 2" squares. ***Note:*** *You will have a small amount of fabric left over.*

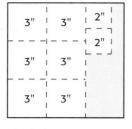

Shaded areas represent unused fabric.

6. Referring to the diagram, fold each of the squares in half. Make sure that the fusible web paper is on the outside. Fold these folded squares in half again. Then fold each square in half one more time on the diagonal, bringing fold to fold to make a triangle. Draw a freehand design on the triangle. Make sure to position some cutout design areas at the folds. To cut out the snowflakes, use the same "paper doll" technique we all learned in grade school; it's helpful to practice on a piece of scrap paper before you actually cut out the snowflakes from fabric. Cut 6 snowflakes from the 3" folded squares and 2 ice crystals from the 2" folded squares. The fusible web paper will remain in place during this step.

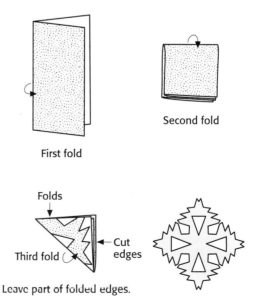

7. Trace the heart pattern A from page 62 onto fusible web. Referring to "Fusible Appliqué" on pages 16–17, fuse the heart shape to the wrong side of a scrap of red fabric. Cut out the heart and place it in the center of one of the snowflakes. Everyone knows that a snowman is born with a magical heart.

8. Referring to page 31, fuse the snowflakes, ice crystals, and heart to the blue background square in random positions. Like snowflakes, there are no two snowmen exactly alike.

block 2

Four Patch Block, Filler I

Finished Size: 10" x 12"

This snowman's album includes snapshots of some of his favorite things—mittens and stockings for warming hands and feet, colorful pine trees, and stars from a winter skyline.

PATTERNS	PIECES	NUMBER OF PIECES
First Rectangle, Stocking	B–B3	1 each
Second Rectangle, Star	C C1	1 5
Third Rectangle, Mitten	D–D3	1 each
Fourth Rectangle, Tree	E–E1	1 each

Directions

1. From a white-on-white print, cut 4 rectangles, each 5" x 6".

2. From a light blue fabric, cut one 1½" x 42" strip. Cut the light blue strip into two 1½" x 5" strips and one 1½" x 13" strip.

3. Referring to "Fusible Appliqué" on pages 16–17, the quilt photo on page 27, and the patterns on page 62, prepare and fuse the appliqué pieces to the 4 white rectangles. ***Note:*** *You will need to reverse the appliqué patterns so that the appliqué pieces face the right way after fusing.*

4. Referring to the diagram, sew the light blue 1½" x 5" strips to the bottom edges of 2 of the rectangles. Sew the remaining 2 rectangles to the bottom of these units.

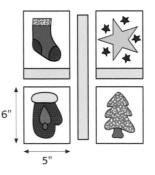

5. Referring to the diagram, sew the light blue 1½" x 13" strip between the two rectangular units to form a Four Patch block. *Note: This strip is slightly longer than necessary to allow for variances in seam allowances. Trim the strip to the appropriate length after the units are joined.*

block 3

A Snowman's First Tree Trimming

Finished Size: 19" x 12"
with filler strips

For our daughter Kristi's first Christmas, we went to a tree farm to pick out a real tree. We lived in New Jersey at the time, where ponds freeze over and there is lots of snow in December. Wanting to dress our little girl warmly for the occasion, we purchased her very first snowsuit at a local department store. It was padded so well that it was difficult for her to lower her arms. This snowman's mom apparently purchased his snowsuit at the same store.

PATTERNS	PIECES	NUMBER OF PIECES
Snowman	F–F7r	1 each
Trees	G–G3	1 each
Bird and Birdhouse	H–H3	1 each
	H4	2

Directions

1. From a blue background fabric, cut a 9½" x 18" rectangle.
2. From a white-on-white print, cut a 2½" x 18" rectangle.
3. Sew the white rectangle to the bottom edge of the blue rectangle to form the background block.
4. Referring to "Fusible Appliqué" on pages 16–17, the quilt photo on page 27, and the patterns on page 63, prepare and fuse the appliqué pieces to the background block. For the earmuffs, you could use small pieces of wool, felt, or fake fur instead of cotton fabric. *Note: You will need to reverse the appliqué patterns so that the appliqué pieces face the right way after fusing.*
5. Referring to the quilt photo and to "Buttonhole Stitch" on page 17, buttonhole stitch around appliqué pieces.
6. Referring to the quilt photo, embroider the facial features and earmuff connecting piece.
7. Embellish the block with small buttons or beads for the snowman's snowsuit. You may also use buttons for the lights on the trees. I used a miniature strand of Christmas lights that I found at a hobby and craft center.
8. Sew an A filler strip to the top of the block. Trim it even with the side edges of the block.
9. Sew an A filler strip to the right side of the block. Trim it even with the top and bottom edges of the block.
10. Trim the filler strips across the top of the block so that the block measures 19½" x 12½".

block 4
A Snowman Fishing

Finished Size: 12" x 12"
with filler strip

When my son, Michael, was small, he liked to put on his red-and-white striped shirt and red thong sandals (his lucky outfit), grab his fishing pole, and head out for an all-day adventure. I took pictures to show everyone just how big the fish really were. I couldn't resist dressing this snowman in the same kind of red-and-white striped shirt and red thongs for his big fishing adventure.

PATTERN	PIECES	NUMBER OF PIECES
Fisherman Snowman	I, I3–I6, I9	1 each
	I1–I2, I7	2 each
	I8	3
	I10	1 and 1 reversed

Directions

1. From a light blue background fabric, cut an 8½" x 12½" rectangle.

2. From the tan fabric, cut a 3" x 12½" rectangle.

3. Sew the tan rectangle to the bottom edge of the light blue rectangle to form the background block.

4. Referring to "Fusible Appliqué" on pages 16–17, iron fusible web to a 2" x 12½" piece of dark blue fabric. Do not remove the paper backing. On a piece of scrap paper, practice drawing some curvy lines for waves. Then draw this wave pattern on the fusible-web paper backing attached to the dark blue strip. Refer to the diagram for additional guidance. Cut along your drawn lines, remove the paper, and position the straight edge of this strip on the seam where the light blue and tan fabrics meet. This creates the water. Fuse the dark blue strip to the background block.

5. Referring to the quilt photo on page 27 and to "Buttonhole Stitch" on page 17, buttonhole stitch the long, straight edge and the curved edge of the water strip in place. *Note: You must do this buttonhole stitching before moving on to the next step, because all other designs are placed on top of the water.*

6. Referring to "Fusible Appliqué," the quilt photo, and the pattern pieces on page 64, prepare and fuse the appliqué pieces to the background block. *Note: You will need to reverse the appliqué patterns so that the appliqué pieces face the right way after fusing.*

7. Buttonhole stitch around all the appliqué pieces *except* the starfish. Referring to "Running Stitch" on page 17, do running stitches around the starfish.

8. Referring to the quilt photo, embroider the facial features, buttons, and tackle line with the floss colors of your choice.

9. Embellish the block as you desire. Some suggestions that I recommend include placing a small stick in one of the snowman's hands for a fishing pole. Try using embroidery floss to represent a fishing line (be sure to use a bright color that will show up against the background fabric). Look for buttons shaped like sea creatures. You can sew these to the quilt top.

10. Sew an A filler strip to the bottom edge of the block. Trim it even with the sides of the block.

block 5

A Snowman Skis the Slopes

Finished Size: 20½" x 14½"
with filler strips

Whenever our family used to take ski trips, I liked to drop everyone off at the ski lift area, make my way to the rest area at the bottom of the slope, order a hot chocolate, and wait with camera in hand for the first family member to come down the slopes. One snowy morning, I became anxious when I saw my son, Michael, who was 10 at the time, sliding toward me on his bottom rather than skiing in an upright position. After making sure there were no broken bones, I asked him what happened. He said, "Oh, my sister took me to a slope with a pretty, black diamond sign." Ski runs with those signs are the most difficult and require advanced levels of skiing ability. This experience made me wonder. What would happen if this snowman had the same type of ski instruction that Michael had from his older sister?

PATTERNS	PIECES	NUMBER OF PIECES
Snowman and Tree	J–J13	1 each

Directions

1. From a blue fabric, cut a 13" x 19" rectangle.
2. From a white-on-white print, cut a 6" x 19" rectangle.
3. Referring to "Fusible Appliqué" on pages 16–17, iron fusible web to the wrong side of the white rectangle. Do not remove the paper backing. On a piece of scrap paper, practice drawing ski slope shapes. Then draw some curved ski slopes on the fusible-web paper backing attached to the white rectangle. Cut along your drawn lines, remove the paper, and fuse the slope piece to the blue rectangle to form the background block. Make sure to align the straight edge of the slope piece with the bottom edge of the blue rectangle.

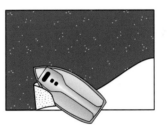

4. Referring to "Fusible Appliqué," the quilt photo on page 27, and the patterns on page 65, prepare and fuse the appliqué pieces to the background block. ***Note:*** *You will need to reverse the appliqué patterns so that the appliqué pieces face the right way after fusing.*
5. Referring to "Buttonhole Stitch" on page 17, stitch around the appliqué pieces.
6. Referring to the quilt photo, embroider facial features.
7. Embellish the block as you desire. I added a ski slope pin that Michael collected on a ski trip. You could also use wooden sticks instead of fabric for the skis, and wool or felt for the snowman's hat and sweater.
8. Sew a B filler strip to the top of the block. Trim the strip even with the side edges of the block.
9. Sew a B filler strip to the right side of the block. Trim the strip even with the top and bottom edges of the block.

block 6

A Snowman's Family Portrait

Finished Size: 29" x 14½"
with filler strip

There is hardly a family anywhere that has not, at one time or another, had a family portrait made where everyone is forced to sit up straight, tilt their heads at a certain angle, and SMILE. This snowman's family is no different. By the way, the cat on the leash in this block is a family joke regarding my husband's aunt, who had a city ordinance passed that required cat owners to keep their cats on a leash when outside.

PATTERNS	PIECES	NUMBER OF PIECES
Tree	J12–J13	1 each
Snowman Family and Trees	K, K2, K6, K9	2 each
	K1, K3–K5, K7–K8, K10–K11r, K13–K18	1 each
	K12	1 and 1 reversed

Directions

1. From a blue background fabric, cut a 13" x 29 ½" rectangle.

2. From a white-on-white print, cut a 4" x 29½" rectangle.

3. Referring to "Fusible Appliqué" on pages 16–17, iron fusible web to the wrong side of the white rectangle. Do not remove the paper backing. As you did for the ski slopes in block #5, practice drawing some curved lines on a piece of scrap paper for ski slopes. Then draw curved ski slopes on the fusible-web paper backing attached to the white rectangle. Cut along your drawn lines, remove the paper, and fuse the slope piece to the blue rectangle to form the background block. Make sure to align the straight edge of the slope piece with the bottom edge of the blue rectangle.

4. Referring to "Fusible Appliqué," the quilt photo on page 27, and the patterns on pages 65–67, prepare and fuse the appliqué pieces to the background block. *Note: You will need to reverse the appliqué patterns so that the appliqué pieces face the right way after fusing.*

5. Referring to "Buttonhole Stitch" on page 17, buttonhole stitch around the appliqué pieces.

6. Referring to the quilt photo, embroider the facial features and other areas marked for embroidery.

7. Embellish the block as you desire. I threaded floss through a small bell to make a collar and leash for the cat. I drew the cat's face, whiskers, and heart with an ultra-fine, fabric-marking pen. I placed a small, red bow in the hair of the snowman's sister and added trim to her skirt.

8. Sew a B filler strip to the bottom edge of the block. Trim it even with the side edges of the block.

block 7
Candy Cane Filler

Finished Size: 3½" x 14½"

There's nothing as wonderful as tasting the sweetness of a candy cane at Christmastime. You can make your candy canes traditional red and white, or try other color combinations like green and white.

PATTERN	PIECE	NUMBER OF PIECES
Candy Cane	L	6

Directions

1. From a white-on-white print, cut a 4" x 15" rectangle.
2. Referring to "Fusible Appliqué" on pages 16–17, the quilt photo on page 27, and the pattern on page 68, prepare and fuse 6 candy cane appliqué pieces to the white rectangle. *Note: You will need to reverse the appliqué patterns so that the appliqué pieces face the right way after fusing.*
3. Referring to "Buttonhole Stitch" on page 17, buttonhole stitch around each candy cane.
4. Sew this block to the right-hand side of block 6.

block 8
A Snowman's Uncle: Jack Frost

Finished Size: 12" x 12"
with filler strip

We live in an area of Oklahoma known as Green Country, where there is a produce farm on almost every other corner. Every year in the fall, grade school children take a field trip to the pumpkin patch, where they are each allowed to pick any pumpkin they can carry and take it home. This is usually about the time that we have the first frost of the year; hence, the saying "The frost is on the pumpkin . . . it won't be long 'til winter." I felt that this snowman's uncle, Jack Frost, should be included in his family album to commemorate this occasion.

PATTERNS	PIECES	NUMBER OF PIECES
Cat	K14	1
Jack Frost and Pumpkins	M–M10	1 each

Directions

1. From a blue background fabric, cut a 10½" x 12½" rectangle.
2. From the brown fabric for ground, cut a 2½" x 10½" rectangle.
3. Referring to "Fusible Appliqué" on pages 16–17, iron fusible web to the wrong side of the brown rectangle. Do not remove the paper backing. Practice drawing the foreground shape on a piece of scrap paper. Then draw the foreground shape on the fusible-web paper backing attached to the brown rectangle. Cut along your drawn lines, but do not fuse the foreground piece to the background block at this time. All of the other designs in the block go behind the piece, so fuse this shape last.
4. Referring to "Fusible Appliqué," the quilt photo on page 27, and the patterns on pages 67–69, prepare and fuse the appliqué pieces to the background block. When I made this block, I used a piece of fabric with preprinted pumpkins on it. If you can't find similar fabric, use the pumpkin patterns on page 69 and arrange them in any order you choose. **Note:** *You will need to reverse the appliqué patterns so that the appliqué pieces face the right way after fusing.*
5. Referring to the quilt photo and to "Buttonhole Stitch" on page 17, buttonhole stitch around the appliqué pieces.
6. Referring to the quilt photo, embroider the facial features. Draw facial features on the cat using an ultra-fine marking pen.
7. Sew a B filler strip to the right side of the block. Trim it even with the top and bottom edges of the block.

block 9

A Snowman's Spring Break

Finished Size: 21" x 12"
with filler strip

Each year during the last week of March, the shores of southern resorts like South Padre, Texas, or Miami Beach, Florida, are inundated with teenagers from all over the country. This migration is commonly referred to as "spring break." As a family, we normally liked to spend our spring-break time skiing, but one year my daughter begged to head south with all her friends. Unfortunately, when this snowman tried the same thing, he found out that his mother really did know best—the cooler climate was better for him.

PATTERNS	PIECES	NUMBER OF PIECES
Snowman, Sun, and Signpost	N–N13	1 each

Directions

1. From a blue background fabric, cut an 8" x 21½" rectangle.
2. From the tan fabric, cut a 3" x 21½" rectangle.
3. Sew the tan rectangle to the bottom edge of the blue rectangle to form the background block.
4. Referring to "Fusible Appliqué" on pages 16–17, the quilt photo on page 27, and the patterns on pages 69–70, prepare and fuse the appliqué pieces to the background block. *Note: You will need to reverse the appliqué patterns so that the appliqué pieces face the right way after fusing.*
5. Referring to the quilt photo and to "Buttonhole Stitch" on page 17, buttonhole stitch around all the appliqué pieces *except* the sun face and postcard. Use a running stitch around the edges of the sun face. Refer to "Running Stitch" on page 17 for instructions.
6. Using an ultra-fine fabric-marking pen, write a note on the postcard and label the ice bag and signpost.
7. Using the stem stitch, create the umbrella handle. Stitch 2 rows, if necessary.
8. Referring to the quilt photo and the patterns, embroider the facial features on the snowman and sun and the words on the postcard and signpost.
9. Sew a B filler strip to the bottom edge of the block. Trim it even with the side edges of the block.

block 10
Four Patch Block, Filler II

Finished Size: 10" x 12"

This Four Patch Filler II block is made the same way as the Four Patch Filler I block. You can use the patterns listed here, or mix and match appliqué pieces on the rectangles in any way you like to customize your snowman quilt.

PATTERNS	PIECES	NUMBER OF PIECES
First Rectangle, Birdhouse	H–H1, H3 H4	1 each 2
Second Rectangle, Moon	02–05	1 each
Third Rectangle, Holly	0 01	3 2
Fourth Rectangle, Tree	E–E1	1 each

Directions

1. From the white-on-white print, cut 4 rectangles, each 5" x 6".
2. From a light blue fabric, cut a 1½" x 42" strip. Cut the light blue strip into two 1½" x 5" strips and one 1½" x 13" strip.
3. Referring to "Fusible Appliqué" on pages 16–17, the quilt photo on page 27, and the patterns on pages 62, 63, and 75, prepare and fuse the appliqué pieces to the 4 white rectangles. *Note: You will need to reverse the appliqué patterns so that the appliqué pieces face the right way after fusing. When you trace the H piece, trace it without the branch by following the dashed lines on the pattern.*
4. Referring to the diagram, sew the light blue 1½" x 5" strips to the bottom edges of 2 of the rectangles. Sew the remaining 2 rectangles to the bottom of these units.

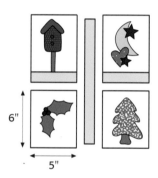

6"

5"

5. Referring to the diagram, sew the light blue 1½" x 13" strip between the 2 rectangular units to form a Four Patch block. *Note: This strip is slightly longer than necessary to allow for variances in seam allowances. Trim the strip to the appropriate length after the units are joined.*

block 11
A Snowman on St. Patrick's Day

Finished Size: 10" x 12"

As children, Kristi and Michael looked forward to St. Patrick's Day. It was the only day of the year that you were allowed to pinch your brother or sister before they pinned on their holiday shamrock. In this block, the snowman is getting ready for a St. Patrick's Day parade with his own shamrocks.

PATTERNS	PIECES	NUMBER OF PIECES
Snowman and Shamrocks	P–P5	1 each

Directions

1. From a blue background fabric, cut a 10½" x 11" rectangle.
2. From the green fabric for grass, cut a 2" x 10½" rectangle.
3. Referring to "Fusible Appliqué" on pages 16–17, iron fusible web to the wrong side of the green rectangle. Fuse the green rectangle to the bottom of the blue rectangle to form the background block. Make sure to align the bottom edge of the green rectangle with the bottom edge of the blue rectangle.

4. Referring to "Fusible Appliqué," the quilt photo on page 27, and the patterns on page 71, prepare and fuse the appliqué pieces to the background block. For this block, I made the snowman from a piece of batting rather than fabric. You can also add shamrocks as desired. *Note: You will need to reverse the appliqué patterns so that the appliqué pieces face the right way after fusing.*

5. Referring to the quilt photo and to "Buttonhole Stitch" on page 17, buttonhole stitch around the appliqué pieces.

6. Referring to the quilt photo, embroider the facial features and snowman's buttons.

block 12

A Snowman Plays Santa

Finished Size: 25½" x 14½"
with filler strips

One of my fondest memories as a child was going to the annual Christmas party at the place where my father worked. He was a welder at a large steel company that rarely did anything for employees, with the exception of the Christmas party. We would all dress up in our Sunday best and climb into my dad's '57 Chevy. The drive downtown always seemed to last forever, but when we finally arrived, the party room was beyond belief. There were lights, garlands, tinsel, and every treat a child could imagine. In one corner was a large sleigh overflowing with packages (one for every

child). The owner of the company dressed as Santa. His fake Santa beard was held in place with an elastic string that stretched around the back of his head. After dutifully handing out every gift, he would pull down his beard and rest it on his chin while he drank egg nog. I do not have a photo of that special time, so I created my own in this block.

PATTERNS	PIECES	NUMBER OF PIECES
Tree	E–E1	1 each
Santa Snowman and Sleigh	Q–Q2, Q4–Q13 Q3	1 each 2

Directions

1. From a blue background fabric, cut a 10" x 23½" rectangle.

2. From a white-on-white print, cut one 3½" x 23½" rectangle.

3. Sew the white rectangle to the bottom of the blue rectangle to form the background block.

4. Referring to "Fusible Appliqué" on pages 16–17, the quilt photo on page 27, and the patterns on pages 62 and 72, prepare and fuse the appliqué pieces to the background block. *Note: You will need to reverse the appliqué patterns so that the appliqué pieces face the right way after fusing.*

5. Referring to the quilt photo and to "Buttonhole Stitch" on page 17, buttonhole stitch around the appliqué pieces.

6. Referring to the quilt photo, embroider the facial features. Use buttons, floss, and strings to represent the elastic on the beard.

7. Embellish the appliqué pieces as you desire. I filled the sleigh with an assortment of buttons. Buttons shaped like a teddy bear and packages would look nice. The more you use, the more stuffed Santa's bag will appear. I decorated the tree with a small garland trim from the miniature section of my local craft store.

8. Sew a B filler strip to the bottom edge of the block. Trim the strip even with the side edges of the block.
9. Sew a B filler strip to the right side of the block. Trim the strip even with the top and bottom edges of the block.

block 13

A Snowman's Aunt: Slim Frost

Finished Size: 10" x 14½"
with filler strip

From the time she was very young, my daughter, Kristi, always wanted to be an actress. She loved to dress up, place a hat on her head, throw a scarf around her neck, and entertain us with various routines. I imagine that this snowman's aunt, Slim Frost (Jack's wife), is also an actress. Over the years, she has maintained her girlish figure so that she can fit into all her costumes. With a scarf draped around her neck and her cap neatly in place, she is ready to perform.

PATTERN	PIECES	NUMBER OF PIECES
Slim Frost	R–R6	1 each

Directions

1. From a blue background fabric, cut a 9" x 15" rectangle.
2. Referring to "Fusible Appliqué" on pages 16–17, the quilt photo on page 27, and the pattern on page 73, prepare and fuse the appliqué pieces to the background block. ***Note:*** *You will need to reverse the appliqué patterns so that the appliqué pieces face the right way after fusing.*
3. Referring to the quilt photo and to "Buttonhole Stitch" on page 17, buttonhole stitch around the appliqué pieces.
4. Referring to the quilt photo, embroider the facial features.
5. Embellish the appliqué pieces as you desire. I added buttons down the front of Slim Frost, a bell to her hat, and an appliquéd heart as the finishing touch. A heart button would also work.
6. Sew an A filler strip to the right side of the block. Trim the strip even with the top and bottom edges of the block.

block 14

A Snowman at Retirement

Finished Size: 18" x 14½"

In today's job market, it is rare that a person stays with a company more than fifteen or twenty years. When my father-in-law retired from Sun Oil Company, he had been an employee for thirty-seven and a half years. The company presented him with the ceremonial gold watch as a symbol of their appreciation. How fitting that at this snowman's retirement, as the winter season came to an end, he, too, had a "gold watch" ceremony.

PATTERN	PIECES	NUMBER OF PIECES
Retirement Snowman	S–S7	1 each

Directions

1. From a blue background fabric, cut one 15" x 19" rectangle.

2. Referring to "Fusible Appliqué" on pages 16–17, the quilt photo on page 27, and the pattern on page 74, prepare and fuse the appliqué designs to the background block. ***Note:*** *The snowman should appear to be melting. You may need to make several narrow layers of white snow with fabric, extending the layers toward the edges of the block to get this effect. You will also need to reverse the appliqué patterns so that the appliqué pieces face the right way after fusing.*

3. Referring to the quilt photo and to "Buttonhole Stitch" on page 17, buttonhole stitch around the appliqué piece.

4. Referring to the quilt photo, embroider the facial features.

5. Embellish this block as you desire. I threaded a piece of gold-colored ribbon through a plastic, gold-colored watch button and attached it to the snowman's arm to represent his retirement as he melted away. Buttons like this are available in various sizes in the miniatures section of craft stores.

Quilt Top Assembly

The "Snowman's Family Album" quilt consists of 4 horizontal rows. Refer to the quilt photo on page 27 and the quilt plan on page 30 for block placement guidance.

(Refer to the quilt photo on page 27 and the quilt plan on page 30)

1. Arrange the blocks into rows. Sew the blocks in each row together. Press all of the seam allowances to one side—either all to the left or all to the right.
2. Join the 4 horizontal rows to make the quilt top.

The Inner Border

The vibrant yellow print in the narrow inner border surrounds the snowman blocks with a hint of bright winter sunshine.

1. From the yellow inner border fabric, cut 6 strips, each 1" x 42".
2. Referring to "Borders" on page 20, join the short ends of the 6 strips together.
3. Referring to "Borders," sew the yellow inner border strips to the quilt top.

The Outer Border

Red-and-white checkerboard squares create the perfect finishing touch for "A Snowman's Family Album" quilt. This border would also look great with other contrasting colors.

1. From the red fabric for the checkerboard border, cut 6 strips, each 2½" x 42".
2. From the white fabric for the checkerboard border, cut 6 strips, each 2½" x 42".
3. Referring to "Four-Patch Units" on page 14, make a total of 116 red-and-white pieced segments, each 2½" x 4½".

4. Sew together 2 border sections containing 27 segments each. Referring to the quilt photo on page 27, alternate the colors. Referring to "Borders," sew these 2 pieced border sections to opposite sides of the quilt top.
5. Sew together 2 border sections containing 31 segments each. Alternate the colors as before. Referring to "Borders," sew these 2 pieced border sections to the remaining 2 sides of the quilt top. *Note: Because the finished quilt measurement is 62", which is not evenly divisible by 4, there will be 2 segments where the reds lie next to each other on 2 sides of the quilt.*

Finishing

1. Referring to "Layering and Basting" on pages 21–22, layer and baste the top with batting and backing.
2. Quilt the top as desired.
3. Referring to "Binding" on pages 24–25, "Sleeves" on page 25, and "Signing a Quilt" on page 26, bind the quilt and add a hanging sleeve. Attach a label to the quilt.

Welcome Winter

Welcome Winter *by Mary M. Covey, 1999, Jenks, Oklahoma, 38½" x 30". When I was little, my mother would go around the house saying, "Mitten, mitten, never a pair." We often found ourselves wearing two colorful but non-matching mittens, but we didn't mind a bit, as long as we were able to go out and play in the snow. The vivid colors of the mittens in this block brighten up a gray winter day.*

blocks

Welcome Winter

Finished Block Size: 8½" x 13½"

PATTERN	PIECES	NUMBER OF PIECES
Snowman	K, K2, K4–K6	1 each

Let It Snow

Finished Block Size: 8½" x 13½"

PATTERN	PIECES	NUMBER OF PIECES
Slim Frost	R–R5	1 each

Mitten, Mitten

Finished Block Size: 8½" x 13½"

PATTERN	PIECES	NUMBER OF PIECES
Mitten	D	3

Materials

42"-wide fabric

½ yd. light blue fabric for background blocks

8 assorted fat quarters of white and colored prints for appliqué and connecting block

8" square of fusible fleece (optional) for snowman

⅓ yd. yellow fabric for inner border

½ yd. bright pink fabric for outer border

⅓ yd. bright green fabric for binding

1¼ yds. fabric for backing and hanging sleeve

34" x 42" piece of batting

½ yd. fusible web

Assorted colors of embroidery floss to match appliqués

Buttons for embellishment

Permanent fabric marker

Note: There are at least 8 different fabrics in varying amounts in this project. In some cases, the reverse side of the fabric may make it seem like there are more. An assortment of 8 different fabrics will be more than enough to complete this project.

Cutting

All measurements include ¼"-wide seam allowances.

From the light blue background fabric, cut:
   2 rectangles, each 14" x 9"
   1 rectangle, 9" x 13¼ "
From a white-on-white print, cut:
   One 2½ " x 14" rectangle
From the assorted prints, cut:
   A total of 14 squares, each 4¾" x 4¾"
   8 rectangles, each 2⅝" x 3⅞"
From the yellow fabric, cut:
   4 strips, each 1½" x 42"
From the bright pink fabric, cut:
   4 strips, each 3½" x 42"

Assembly

1. Referring to "Fusible Appliqué" on pages 16–17, iron fusible web to the wrong side of the white rectangle. Do not remove the paper backing. Practice drawing some slopes on a piece of scrap paper. Then draw a curved slope on the fusible-web paper backing attached to the white rectangle. Cut on the line of the slope. Referring to the quilt photo on page 45, remove the paper backing and fuse the slope piece to a 14" x 9" light blue background block. Align the lower straight edge of the slope piece with the bottom edge of the background block.

2. Referring to "Fusible Appliqué," the quilt photo, and the patterns on pages 62, 67, and 73, prepare and fuse the appliqué pieces to each of the 3 background blocks. Use the 14" x 9"

rectangles for Welcome Winter and Mitten, Mitten, and the 9" x 13¼" for the Let It Snow block. For the snowman in Welcome Winter, I cut a piece of fusible fleece the same size as the fabric body piece and fused the fleece to the fabric body. *Note: You will need to reverse the appliqué patterns so that the appliqué pieces face the right way after fusing.*

3. Referring to the quilt photo and to "Buttonhole Stitch" on page 17, buttonhole stitch around the appliqué pieces. Match the floss colors to the fabrics.

4. Referring to the quilt photo and to the lettering patterns on page 78, transfer the lettering to the background blocks. If the background fabric is light, lay it over the patterns and trace the lettering directly onto the fabric with a fine-line mechanical pencil. If the fabric is dark, place the lettering on top of a light box, and lay the dark fabric on top of the lettering patterns to trace them.

5. Referring to "Embellishments" on pages 17–19, backstitch or stem stitch the lettering with 3 strands of a dark floss. Embroider the facial features and snowman's buttons on the Welcome Winter block. If you like, substitute small twigs or couched ribbon for the snowman's arms. Add decorative rickrack, lace, or trim to the top of the mittens on the Mitten, Mitten block.

6. Referring to the diagram, sew together 4 of the 2⅝" x 3⅞" rectangles to form a row. Make 2 of these rows.

Make 2.

7. Sew one of the rows from step 6 to the bottom edge of the Welcome Winter block. Sew the other row from step 6 to the top of the Mitten, Mitten block. After both rows are attached, sew these 2 blocks together to form Unit 1.

14"

Unit 1

8. Referring to the diagram, sew together 2 of the 4¾" x 4¾" squares to form a row. Make 2 of these rows.

Make 2.

9. Sew 1 row from step 8 to the top and 1 row from step 8 to the bottom edges of the Let It Snow block. This will form Unit 2.

Unit 2

10. Sew together 5 of the assorted 4¾" x 4¾" squares together to form a vertical row. Make 2 of these rows.

Make 2.

11. Referring to the quilt photo, sew Unit 1, Unit 2, and the 2 vertical rows from step 10 together to form the "Welcome Winter" quilt.

The Inner Border

1. Referring to "Borders" on page 20, sew 2 yellow inner border strips to opposite sides of the quilt.

2. Referring to "Borders," sew the 2 remaining yellow inner borders to the top and bottom edges of the quilt.

The Outer Border

1. Referring to "Borders," sew 2 bright pink outer border strips to 2 opposite sides of the quilt.

2. Referring to "Borders," sew the 2 remaining bright pink outer border strips to the top and bottom edges of the quilt.

Finishing

1. Referring to "Layering and Basting" on pages 21–22, layer and baste the quilt top, batting, and backing.

2. Quilt as you desire. I machine quilted this quilt completely with the wind swirl design on page 78. I quilted the inner border and blue background in average-size stipple quilting and the larger squares with the snow flower design on page 76. I quilted the snow and snow people in free-motion swirls and ridges.

3. Referring to "Binding" on pages 24–25, "Sleeves" on page 25, and "Signing a Quilt" on page 26, bind the quilt and add a hanging sleeve. Attach a label to the quilt.

4. Sew buttons onto the snow woman on the Let It Snow block. Use assorted sizes and colors. You may substitute a heart button for the heart appliqué piece if you like.

Snowtime Swag

Snowtime Swag *by Mary M. Covey, 1999, Jenks, Oklahoma.*
Hang these charming swags over a doorway, above your mantel, or anywhere they would drape or hang nicely. You can make them as long as you like, simply by adding more blocks. The redwork swag on page 51, which has blocks joined on top of each other, works well in a long, narrow space.

Finished Block Size: 7" x 8"

Materials

42"-wide fabric

⅓ yd. white fabric for background rectangles
8 fat quarters of assorted prints for borders and
    appliqué pieces
⅓ yd. fabric for backing
⅓ yd. lightweight batting or fleece
¼ yd. fusible web
10 buttons in assorted colors
Embroidery floss in red and to match appliqué
    pieces
Permanent fabric marker

Cutting

*All measurements
include ¼"-wide seam allowances.*

From the white fabric, cut:
    5 rectangles, each 5" x 6"
From each of the fat quarters, cut:
    2 strips, each 1¾" x 21"
From one of the fat quarters, cut:
    2 strips, each 1½" x 21"
From the backing fabric, cut:
    5 rectangles, each 7½" x 8½"
    2 strips, each 1½" x 21"
From the lightweight batting or fleece, cut:
    5 rectangles, each 7½" x 8½"

Assembly

1. To make the appliqué swag, refer to "Fusible Appliqué" on pages 16–17, the photo on page 50, and the patterns on page 62. Prepare and fuse the appliqué designs to the white rectangles. *Note: You will need to reverse the appliqué patterns so that the appliqué pieces face the right way after fusing.*

2. Referring to the quilt photo and to "Buttonhole Stitch" on page 17, buttonhole stitch around the appliqué pieces. Match the floss colors to the fabrics. Complete all buttonhole stitching before going to step 3.

3. Sew a 1¾"-wide print border strip to the 2 opposite long sides of a white rectangle. Trim these strips even with the top and bottom edges of the block, and press the seam allowances toward the border strips. Each strip can be used on more than one rectangle.

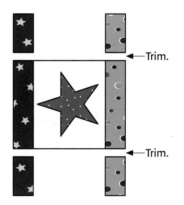

4. In the same manner, sew a 1¾"-wide print border strip to the top and bottom edges of the white rectangle. Trim these strips even with the side edges of the block, and press the seam allowances toward the border strips, as before. *Note: Use a different color fabric for each border so that no two border strips in the block are alike.*

PATTERNS	PIECES	NUMBER OF PIECES
Stocking	B–B3	1 each
Star	C	2 (two blocks with this pattern)
Mitten	D–D3	1 each
Tree	E–E1	1 each

5. Repeat steps 1 through 4 for the remaining 4 white rectangles.

6. With right sides together, place each appliqué block on top of a 7½ x 8½" backing rectangle. Then place a 7½" x 8½" piece of lightweight batting or fleece on top of the block.

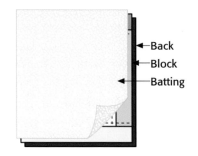

7. Stitch the 3 layers together, leaving a large enough opening on one side for turning. Turn the block right side out and press it. Whipstitch the opening closed by hand.

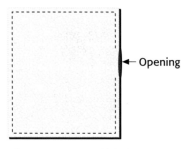

Stitch ¼" seam around block.

8. Machine quilt in the ditch around the borders. Stipple-quilt the background areas and outline-quilt around the appliqué pieces. For a more primitive country look, quilt in the ditch around the border by hand with 2 strands of floss and a large running stitch.

9. For a decorative touch, sew a button to each corner of the blocks.

10. Arrange the blocks in the order you prefer, and tack them together with floss to form a swag.

11. Fold one of the 1½" x 21" strips of fabric in half. Sew the fold to the upper left corner of the first block. Sew the second 1½" x 21" strip to the upper right corner of the last block. Tie these strips to form bows.

12. To make a vertical redwork swag, use embroidery stitches for the designs rather than appliquéing the background blocks. Referring to "Stem Stitch" on page 18, embroider the designs with red floss. Follow steps 3 to 10 to complete the redwork swag, and sew the 1½" x 21" strips to the left and right corners of the top block.

Wanted—One Magic Top Hat!

Wanted—One Magic Top Hat! *by Mary M. Covey, 1999, Jenks, Oklahoma, 38" x 25". The magic top hat is what makes a snowman come to life. Use lively colors to make your quilt come to life, too, and create this cheerful, childlike design.*

Finished Quilt Size: 38" x 25"

PATTERNS	PIECES	NUMBER OF PIECES
Trees	G, G3	1 and 1 reversed (each pattern piece)
	G1–G2	2 and 1 reversed (each pattern piece)
Snowman Knit Hat	V–V2	3 each
Snowman Top Hat	K4	1
Snowman	K	1
Snowman Arms	S6, S6r	1 each
Moon and Stars	O2	1
	O3	4
	O5	5
Banner	T	1

Materials

42"-wide fabric

¼ yd. white-on-white print for snow and snowman

½ yd. light blue fabric for background

8 fat quarters of assorted prints for appliqué pieces and inner border

8" square of fusible or regular fleece

1⅝ yds. orange fabric for middle border, backing, binding, and hanging sleeve

½ yd. dark blue fabric for outer border

29" x 42" piece of batting

½ yd. fusible web

Assorted colors of embroidery floss to match appliqué pieces

Permanent fabric marker

Note: There are at least 8 different fabrics in varying amounts in this project. In some cases the reverse side of the fabric may make it seem like there are more. An assortment of 8 different fabrics will be more than enough to complete this project.

Cutting

All measurements include ¼"-wide seam allowances.

From the white-on-white print, cut:
    A 4" x 27½" rectangle
    4 squares, each 2" x 2"
From the light blue background fabric, cut:
    A 14½" x 27½" rectangle
From the assorted fat quarters, cut:
    8 strips, each 2" x 7¼"
    4 strips, each 2" x 7½"
From the orange fabric, cut:
    4 strips, each 1½" x 42"
From the dark blue fabric, cut:
    4 strips, each 3½ " x 42"
From the fusible web, cut:
    A 4" x 27½" rectangle

Assembly

1. Referring to "Fusible Appliqué" on pages 16–17, fuse the 4" x 27½" piece of fusible web to the wrong side of the white-on-white 4" x 27½" rectangle. Do not remove the paper backing. On a piece of scrap paper, practice drawing some snow mounds. Then draw the shape of the snow mounds on the fusible-web paper backing attached to the white rectangle. Cut on the curved line of the snow mounds.

2. Fuse the white-on-white snow piece to the light blue background block. *Note: Align the straight edge of the white fabric with the bottom of the light blue background block before fusing.*

3. Referring to the patterns on pages 63, 66, 74, and 75, prepare and fuse the appliqué pieces to the background block. Place the appliqué pieces on the block in any order you like. If you want your quilt design to be like the model, refer to the photo of the quilt for placement. For the snowman, you can cut a piece of fusible fleece the same size as the fabric body piece and fuse the fleece to the fabric body (piece K) before buttonhole stitching around the edges. *Note: You will need to reverse the appliqué patterns so that the appliqué pieces face the right way after fusing.*

4. Referring to "Buttonhole Stitch" on page 17, stitch around the appliqué pieces except the stars and snowman's arms.

5. Referring to "Running Stitch" on page 17, do running stitches on the stars and the snowman's arms.

6. Using a permanent fabric-marking pencil, write in the lettering on the banner: "Wanted—one magic top hat!"

7. Referring to "Stem Stitch" on page 18, stitch the lettering on the banner with a dark-colored floss. I used a variegated navy blue color.

8. Referring to the quilt photo, embroider the facial features and snowman's buttons.

9. To make the snowman's scarf, tear a piece of fabric ½" wide and 6" long, so that the edges will be slightly frayed. Find the center of this piece of fabric and stitch the scarf to the snowman with a few small tack stitches. Tie a double knot in the scarf fabric to cover the stitches. Enhance the three-dimensional look of the scarf by using a few tacking stitches at different spots to hold the shape in place. Trim the ends to a length that pleases you.

10. Referring to "Fusible Appliqué" and the patterns on pages 66 and 75, prepare 3 knit hats and 1 top hat, and fuse them to the top of the four 2" x 2" white squares.

11. Referring to the quilt photo and to "Buttonhole Stitch," buttonhole stitch around the appliqué pieces.

The Inner Border

1. Sew 2 of the 2" x 7½" strips together to form a unit. Make 2 of these units. Sew 1 unit to the right side of the background block and 1 to the left side.

2. Sew 4 of the 2" x 7¼" strips together to form a unit. Next, sew a 2" x 2" white square with a knit hat appliqué to each end of this unit. Sew this unit to the bottom edge of the background block.

3. Repeat step 2 to sew the top border, sewing a 2" x 2" white square with a top hat to the right side of the unit and a white square with a knit hat to the left side. Sew this unit to the top edge of the background block.

The Middle and Outer Borders

1. Referring to "Borders" on page 20, sew the orange middle border strips to the quilt.

2. Referring to "Borders," sew the dark blue outer border strips to the quilt.

Finishing

1. Referring to "Layering and Basting" on pages 21–22, layer and baste the quilt top, batting, and backing.

2. Quilt the quilt top as you desire. I machine quilted this quilt completely, but you could hand quilt it. I used an average-size stipple-quilting pattern in the blue background and the 2 inside borders. I quilted the outer border with the wind swirl design on page 78. I free-motion quilted the snow and snowman to create swirls and ridges.

3. Referring to "Binding" on pages 24–25, "Sleeves" on page 25, and "Signing a Quilt" on page 26, bind the quilt and add a hanging sleeve and label.

Winter Is for the Birds

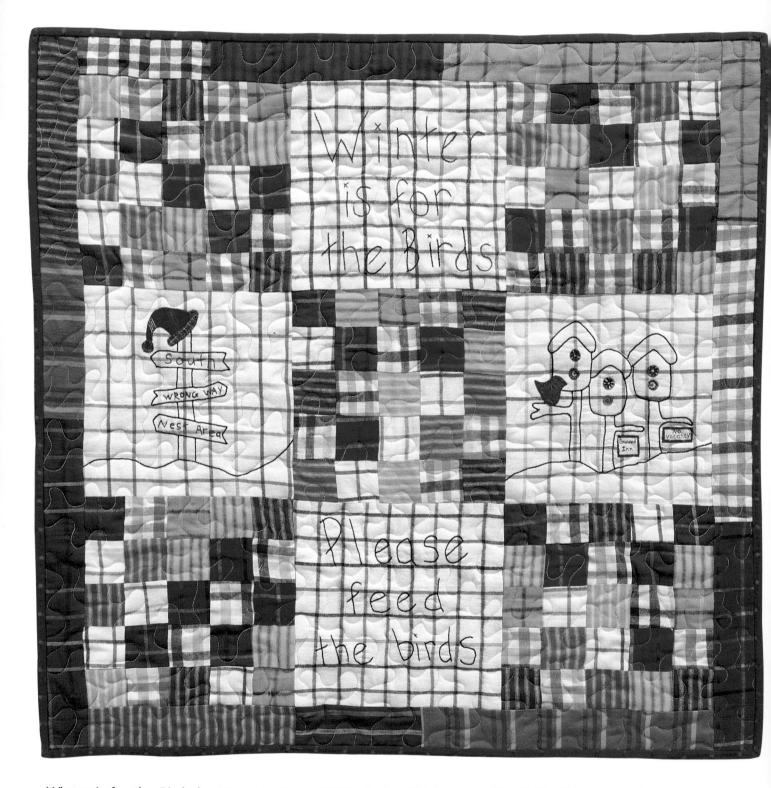

Winter Is for the Birds *by Mary M. Covey, 1999, Jenks, Oklahoma, 34" x 34". Oklahoma, which is where I live, rarely gets snow. When we do, however, things can come to a standstill, with school closings and hazardous driving conditions. It's common to hear a phrase like, "Winter is for the birds," but I love winter, when the snow makes everything look clean and crisp and the air smells fresh, like something out of a storybook.*

blocks

Winter Is for the Birds

Finished Block Size: 10" x 10"

South

Finished Block Size: 10" x 10"

PATTERN	PIECES	NUMBER OF PIECES
Santa Snowman Hat	Q6–Q8	1 each

Snowed Inn

Finished Block Size: 10" x 10"

PATTERNS	PIECES	NUMBER OF PIECES
Bird	U4	1
Birdhouse	H4	6
Signs	U–U3	1 each

Please Feed the Birds

Finished Block Size: 10" x 10"

Twenty-Five Patch Block

(make 5)

Finished Block Size: 10" x 10"

Materials

42"-wide fabric

2 fat quarters of light-colored plaid fabric for appliquéd/embroidered blocks
10 fat quarters of assorted light and dark striped and plaid fabrics for pieced blocks and outer border
Assorted scraps of fabric for appliqué pieces
⅓ yd. dark red fabric for binding
1¼ yds. fabric for backing and hanging sleeve
38" x 38" piece of batting
⅛ yd. fusible web
Assorted colors of floss for embroidery
Permanent fabric marker

Cutting

All measurements include ¼"-wide seam allowances.

Refer to "Rotary Cutting" on pages 12–13 for cutting the following pieces.

1. From the 2 fat quarters of light-colored plaid fabric, cut 4 squares, each 10½" x 10½".
2. Cut the 10 assorted fat quarters of light and dark striped and plaid fabrics into strips that measure 2½" x 21". Start by cutting 2 strips from each piece of fabric; depending on how you decide to mix and match them for the Twenty-Five Patch block, cut more strips as necessary.

Assembly

1. To piece the Twenty-Five Patch block, use the light and dark 2½" x 21" strips to form 2 units. Referring to the diagram, sew together Unit 1 and Unit 2. In each unit, alternate light- and dark-colored strips. Unit 1 begins and ends with a light strip. Unit 2 begins and ends with a dark strip.

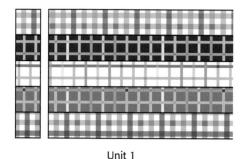

Unit 1

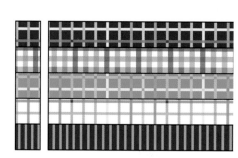

Unit 2

2. Referring to "Rotary Cutting" on pages 12–13, cut Unit 1 and Unit 2 into segments, each 2½" wide.

3. Referring to the previous diagram, sew 2 Unit 1 segments and 3 Unit 2 segments together to form the Twenty-Five Patch block. Make 5 of these Twenty-Five Patch blocks.

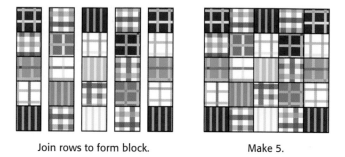

Join rows to form block.   Make 5.

4. Trace the embroidery designs and letters on pages 76–78 onto the 10½" x 10½" squares. Because the background fabric is light, you can lay it over the lettering and designs and trace it directly onto the fabric with a light, fine-line pencil.

5. Referring to "Stem Stitch" on page 18, embroider the designs on the light 10½" x 10½" squares with a dark-colored floss.

6. Referring to "Fusible Appliqué" on pages 16–17, the quilt photo, and the patterns on pages 76–77, prepare and fuse the appliqué pieces to the embroidered squares. *Note: You will need to reverse the appliqué patterns so that the appliqué pieces face the right way after fusing.*

7. Referring to "Buttonhole Stitch" on page 17, buttonhole stitch around all of the appliqué pieces *except* the 2 signs on the Snowed Inn block.

8. Referring to "Running Stitch" on page 17, do running stitches around the 2 signs on the Snowed Inn block.

9. Use a fine-point, permanent fabric-marking pen to write the words *Snowed Inn* and *No Vacancy* on the 2 signs.

10. Referring to the quilt photo for placement, join the pieced and appliquéd/embroidered blocks into 3 rows. Sew the 3 rows together to form the top.

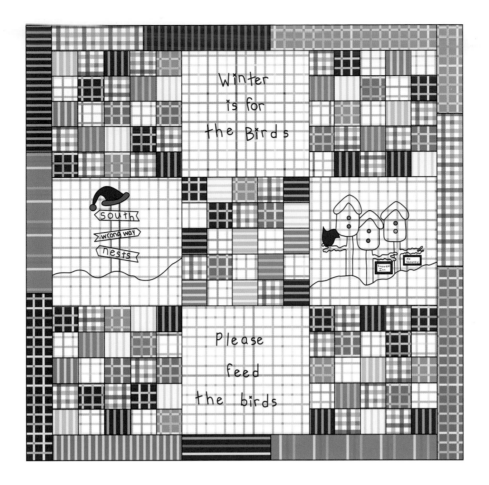

The Outer Border

1. Cut the 2½" x 21" assorted strips into various lengths. Randomly combine them to make 4 pieced outer border strips.
2. Referring to "Borders" on page 20, sew the outer border strips to the top. Trim the strips even with the edges of the top as necessary.

Finishing

1. Referring to "Layering and Basting" on pages 21–22, layer and baste the top with batting and backing.
2. Quilt this top as you desire. I used a medium-size pattern of machine stipple quilting for this project.
3. Referring to "Binding" on pages 24–25, "Sleeves" on page 25, and "Signing a Quilt" on page 26, bind the quilt and add a hanging sleeve. Attach a label to the quilt.

More Snowman Options

You can use the *A Snowman's Family Album Quilt* designs for making other decorative items or accessories. Whether you choose to make something as simple as a place mat or a more detailed project like a vest, your quilted items will add new dimension to your winter stitching repertoire. The design possibilities are endless. Here are just a few of the creative ways you can use snowman designs.

Tote Bags

You can either make your own tote bag with your favorite pattern or start with a purchased tote bag. Fuse the snowman designs of your choice to the bag, and machine appliqué around the edges of each piece. Another idea would be to use your favorite fabric paint pens to outline the edges. Use a hot glue gun to add embellishments and secure them in place.

Pillows

You can make any of the snowman quilt blocks into a beautiful pillow—simply add a border to the block before adding the pillow backing. The following steps describe the process.

1. For a pillow top, make the snowman quilt block of your choice, referring to the instructions for that block.
2. Add a border in whatever size you like. For the pillow top backing, cut a piece of fabric that is 3" larger on each side than the pillow top. Cut a piece of fleece that is also 3" larger than the pillow top. Referring to "Layering and Basting" on pages 21–22, baste the pillow top, fleece, and pillow top backing together.
3. Referring to "Hand Quilting" or "Machine Quilting" on pages 22–24, quilt the pillow top as you desire. Trim the fleece and backing fabric even with the edges of the pillow top.
4. For the back of the pillow, cut a square of fabric that is the same size as the pillow top.
5. If you want to add cording or a ruffle to the pillow top, add them at this time.
6. With right sides together, sew the back pillow fabric to the pillow top. Leave a large enough opening at the bottom edge so that you can insert polyester fiberfill. Turn the pillow right side out, carefully pushing the corners outward. Stuff the pillow with polyester fiberfill, and sew the opening closed by hand.

Single-Block Wall Hangings

How many times have you needed a last minute gift idea for that special friend? This is a quick and easy way to showcase your favorite block. Choose a block and add a small border. Next, layer backing, batting, and the top. Quilt as desired and add binding to create a charming wall hanging. Whether you make only one or many versions of a project, personalize each item with your own style of embellishment.

Gift Bags or Boxes

Snowman block designs make great one-of-a-kind gift bags and boxes. Instead of background fabric, fuse appliqué pieces to paper gift bags or papier-maché boxes, which are readily available at hobby and craft stores. With a pen, draw stitch marks into the designs. For instructions on appliqué, refer to "Fusible Appliqué" on pages 16–17. Add buttons and trim with a glue gun or tacky glue.

Vests and Sweatshirts

Prepare for winter in style by decorating a purchased sweatshirt or vest. Fuse your favorite snowman block designs to a ready-to-wear vest or sweatshirt. Buttonhole stitch around the pieces and embellish the designs as desired. With this technique, you can transform a plain garment into a work of art in no time at all.

Place Mats

The kitchen is usually the center of activity in any household, so include this important room in your winter decorating and fuse some snowman designs to plain, purchased place mats. Either buttonhole stitch the edges of the pieces, or zigzag stitch around the shapes with a sewing machine.

Patterns

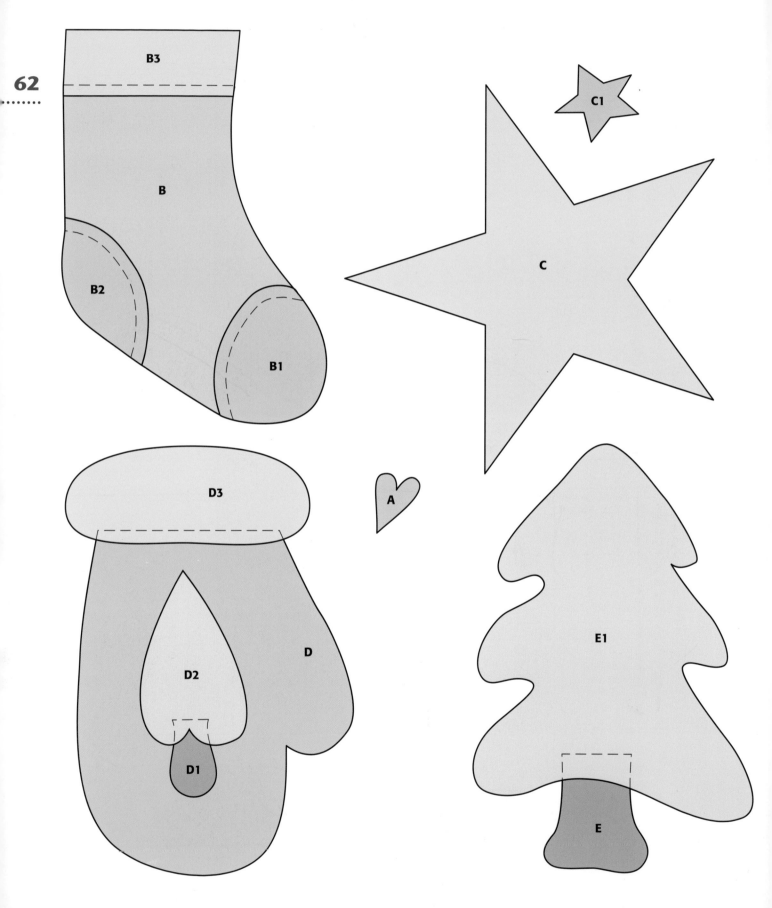

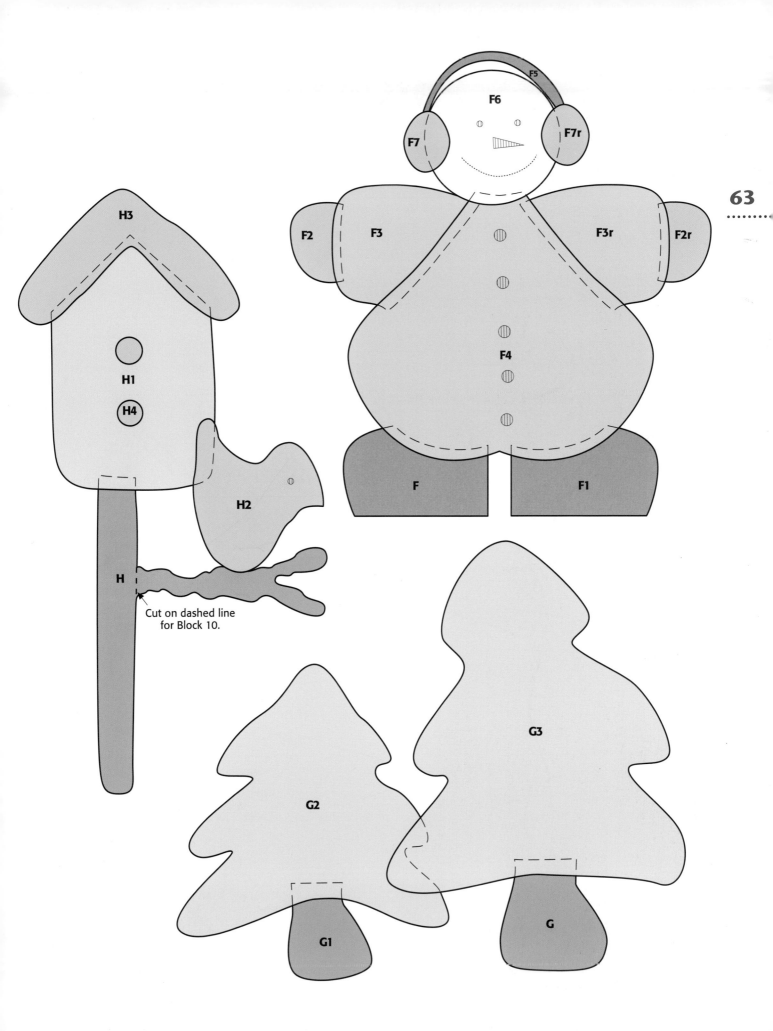

H3

H1

H4

H2

H

Cut on dashed line
for Block 10.

F5

F6

F7

F7r

F2

F3

F3r

F2r

F4

F

F1

G3

G2

G1

G

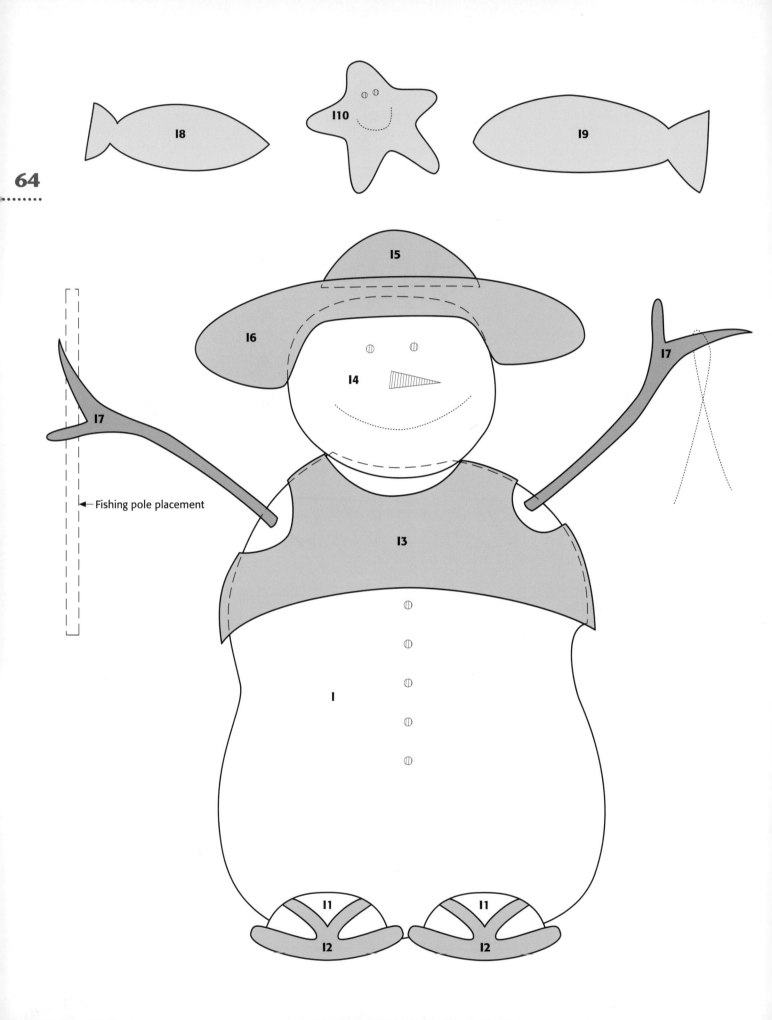

I8

I10

I9

I5

I6

I7

I4

I7

← Fishing pole placement

I3

I

I1

I1

I2

I2

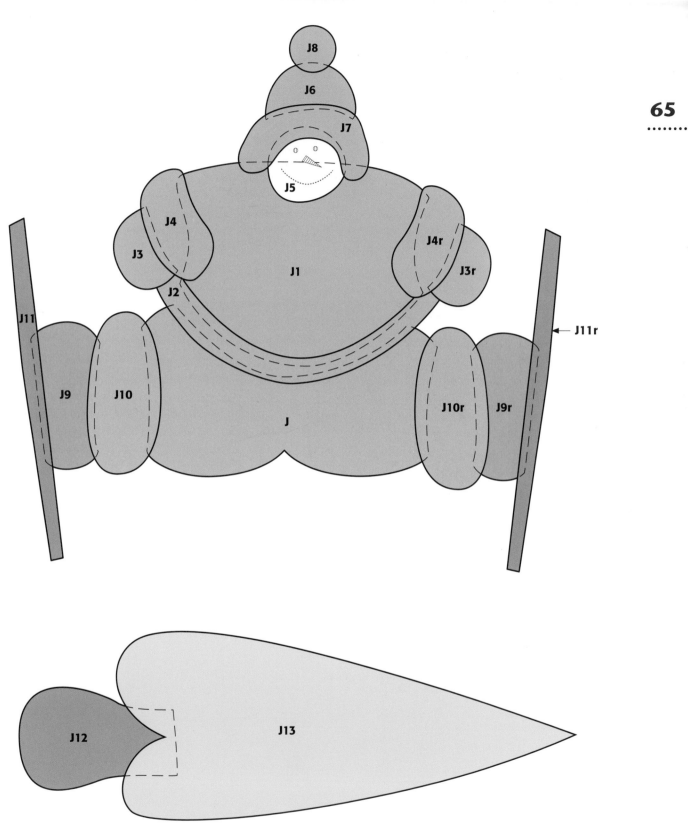

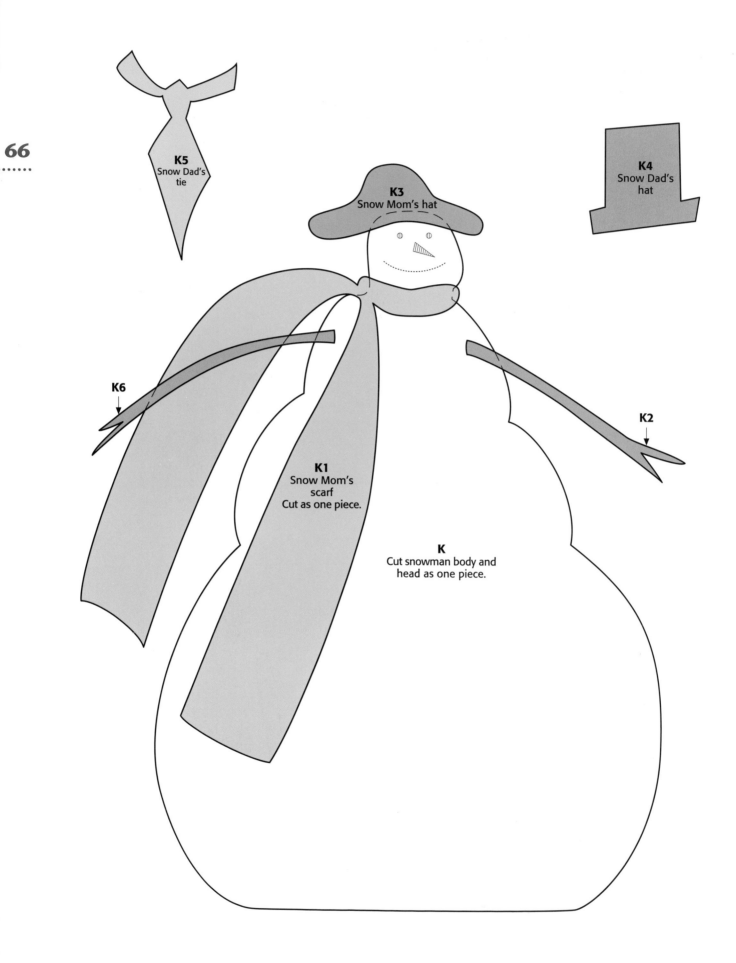

K5
Snow Dad's tie

K3
Snow Mom's hat

K4
Snow Dad's hat

K6

K2

K1
Snow Mom's scarf
Cut as one piece.

K
Cut snowman body and
head as one piece.

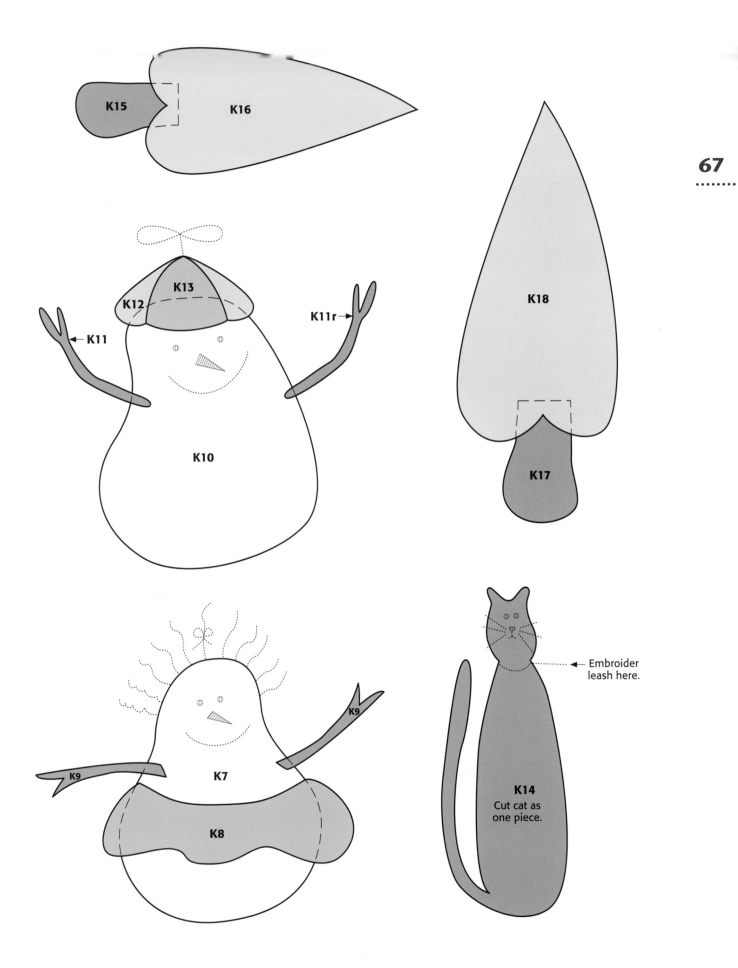

K15

K16

K13

K12

K11r→

←K11

K10

K18

K17

K9

K9

K7

K8

K14
Cut cat as
one piece.

← Embroider
leash here.

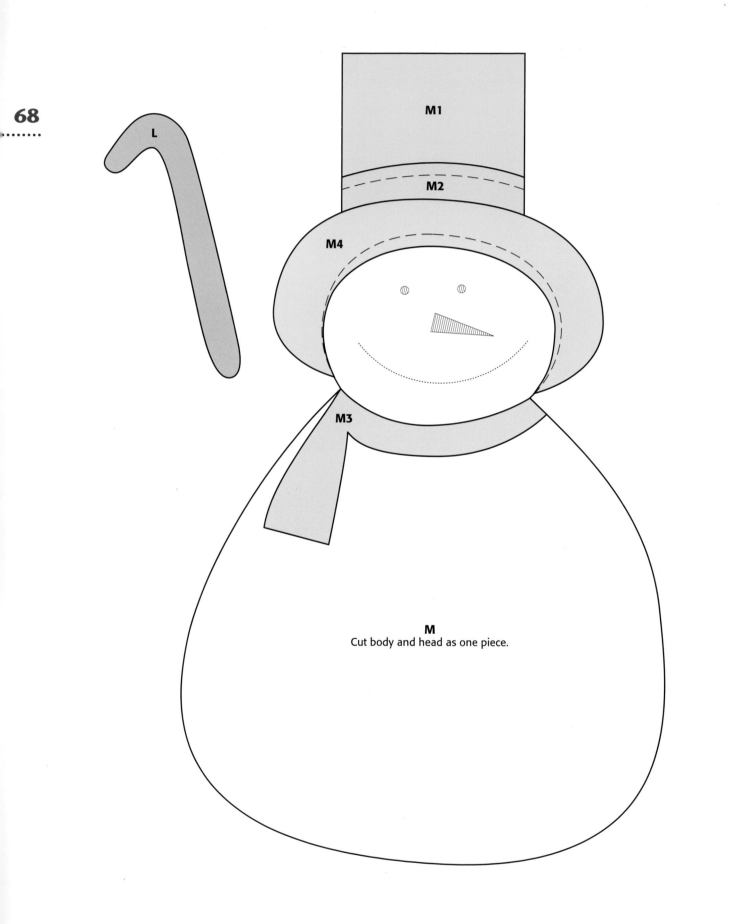

L

M1

M2

M4

M3

M
Cut body and head as one piece.

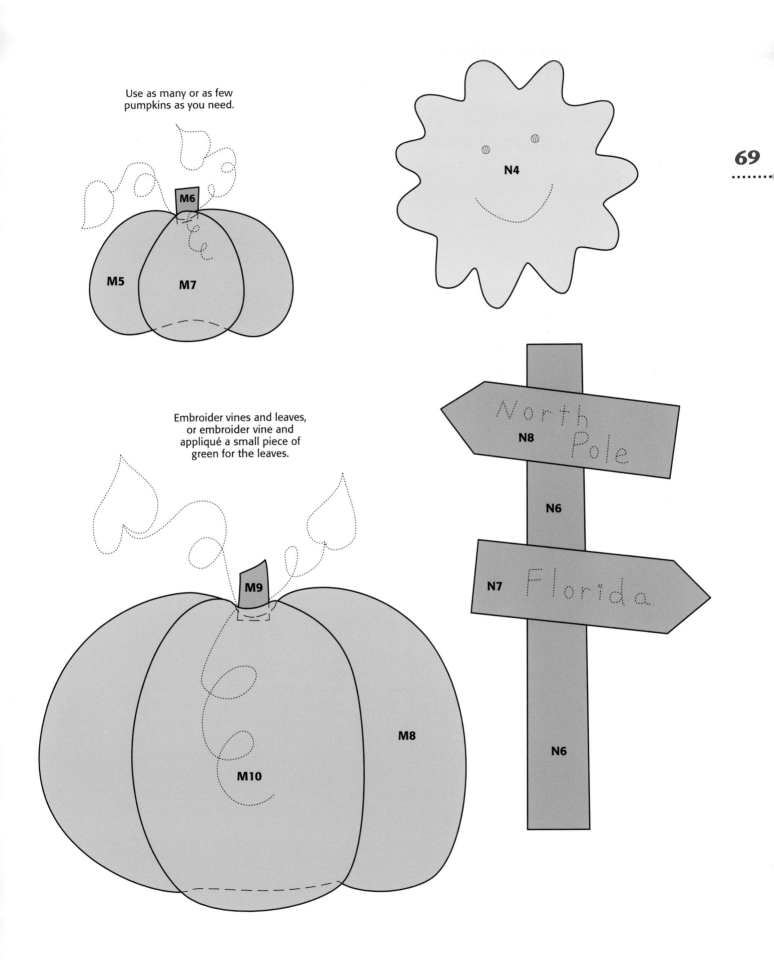

Use as many or as few
pumpkins as you need.

M6

M5   M7

N4

Embroider vines and leaves,
or embroider vine and
appliqué a small piece of
green for the leaves.

M9

M8

M10

North
Pole
N8

N6

N7   Florida

N6

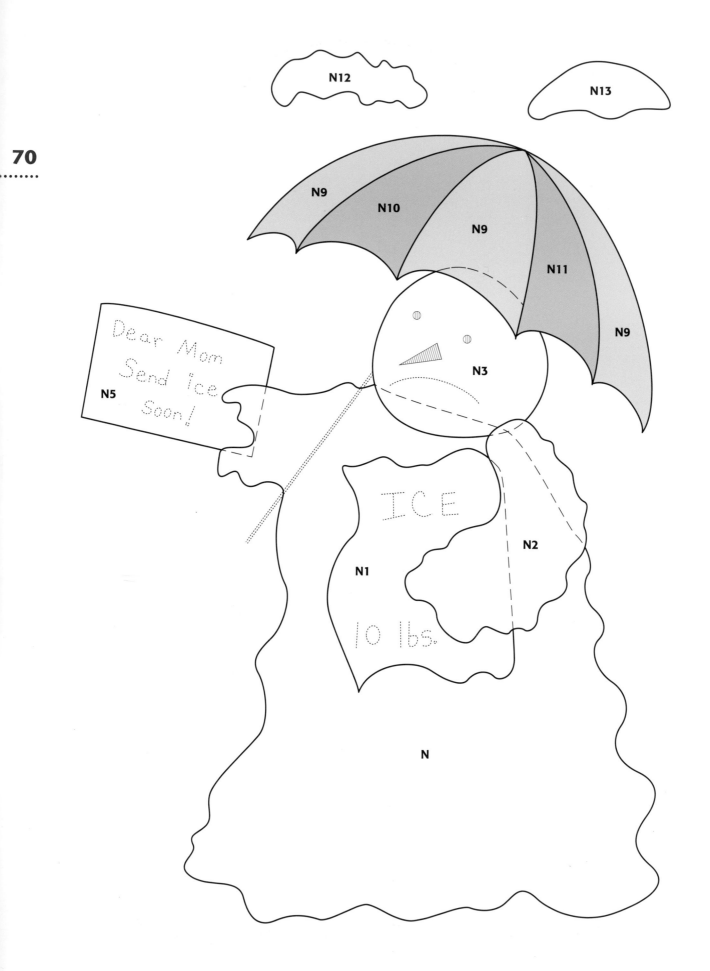

P5

P3

P4

P2

P
Cut body and head
as one piece.

P1

P1r

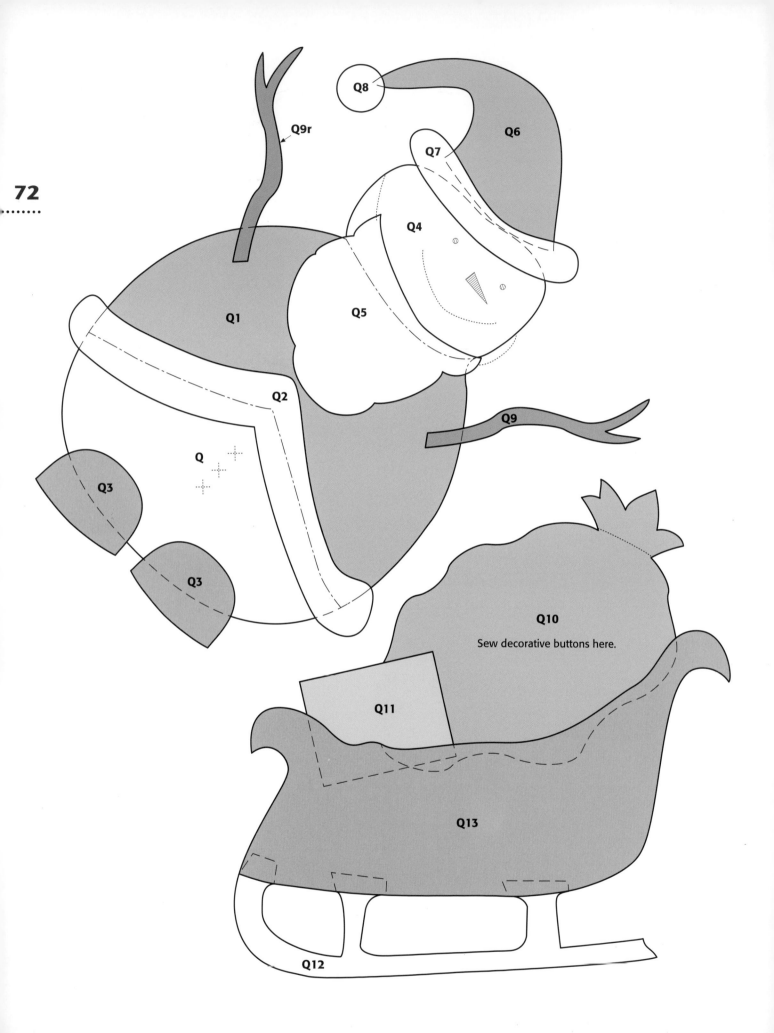

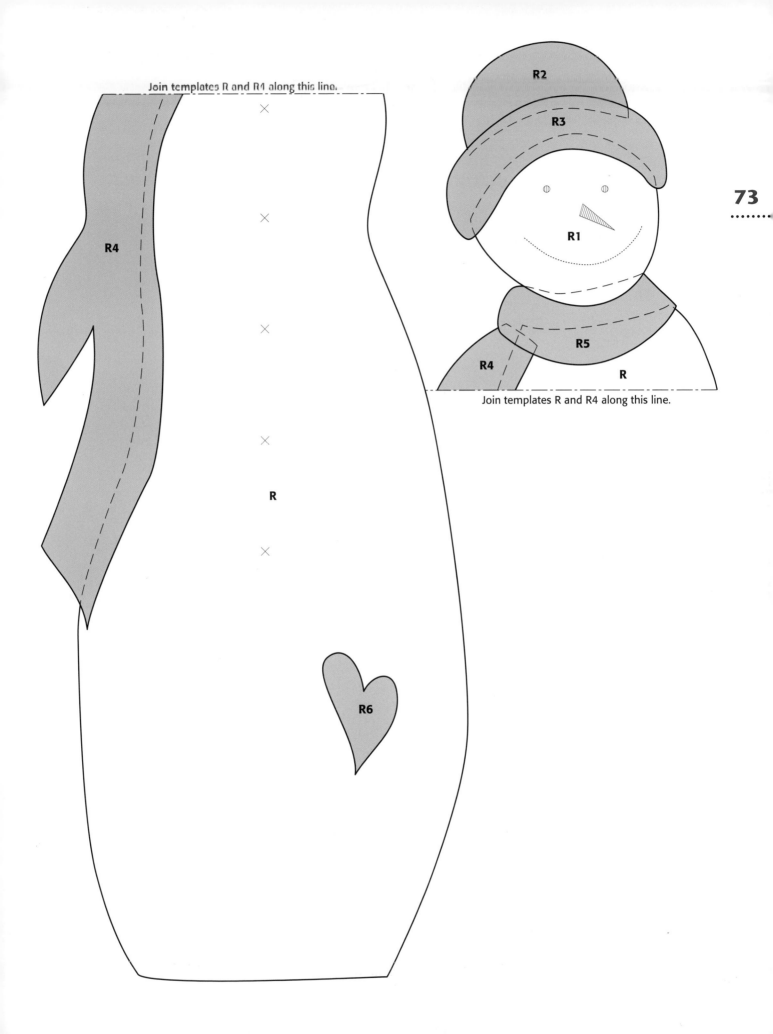

Join templates R and R4 along this line.

R4

R

R2

R3

R1

R5

R4

R

Join templates R and R4 along this line.

R6

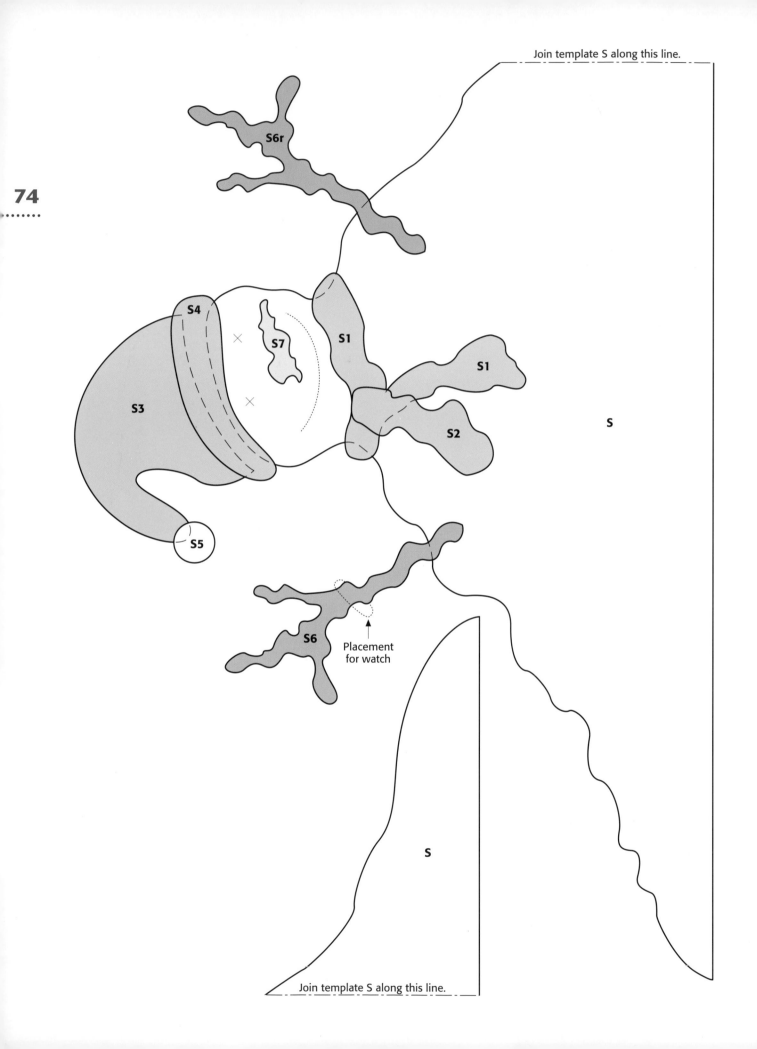

Join template S along this line.

S6r

S4

S7

S1

S1

S3

S2

S

S5

S6

Placement
for watch

S

Join template S along this line.

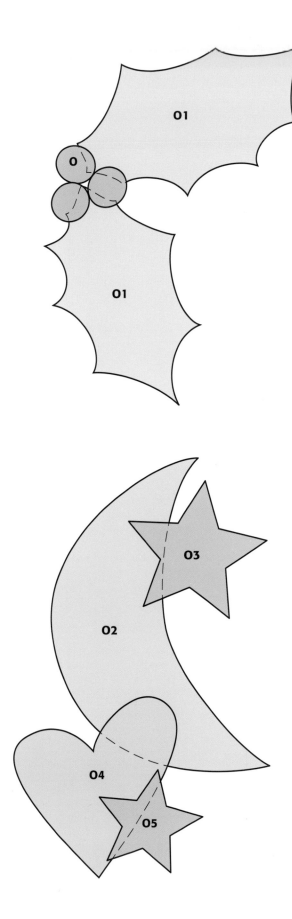

O1

O1

O

O3

O2

O4

O5

T

Wanted — One Magic Top Hat

V2

V

V1

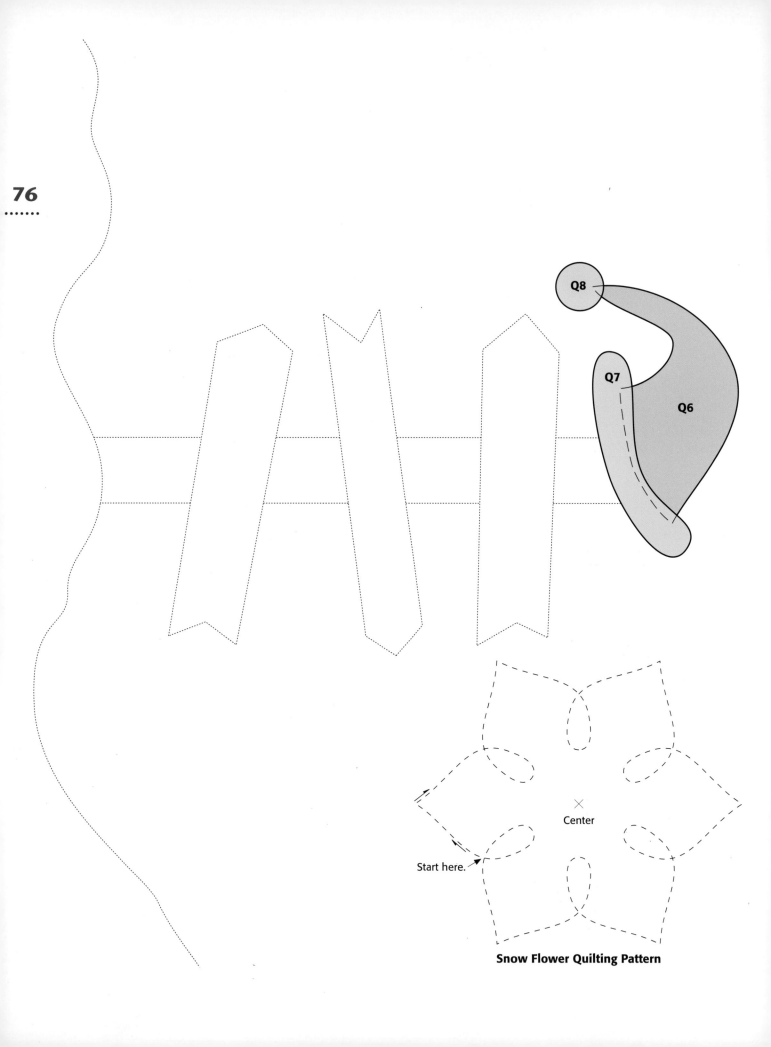

Q8

Q7

Q6

Center

Start here.

Snow Flower Quilting Pattern

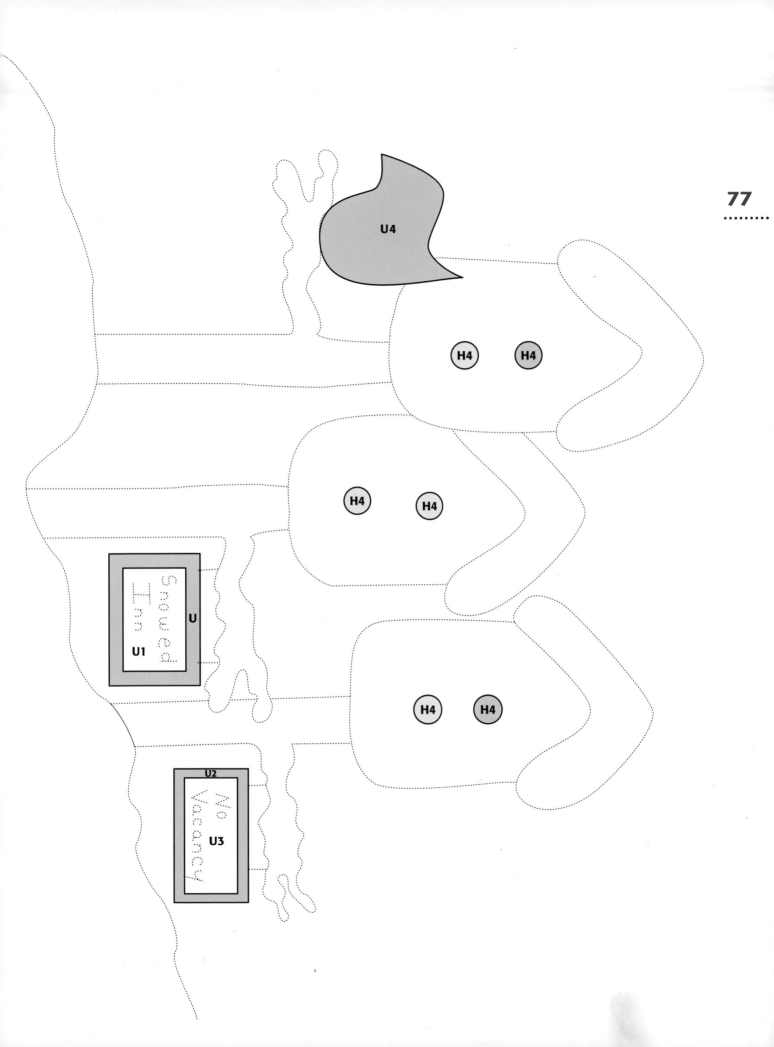

U4

H4 H4

H4 H4

H4 H4

U

U1

Snowed Inn

U2

U3

No Vacancy

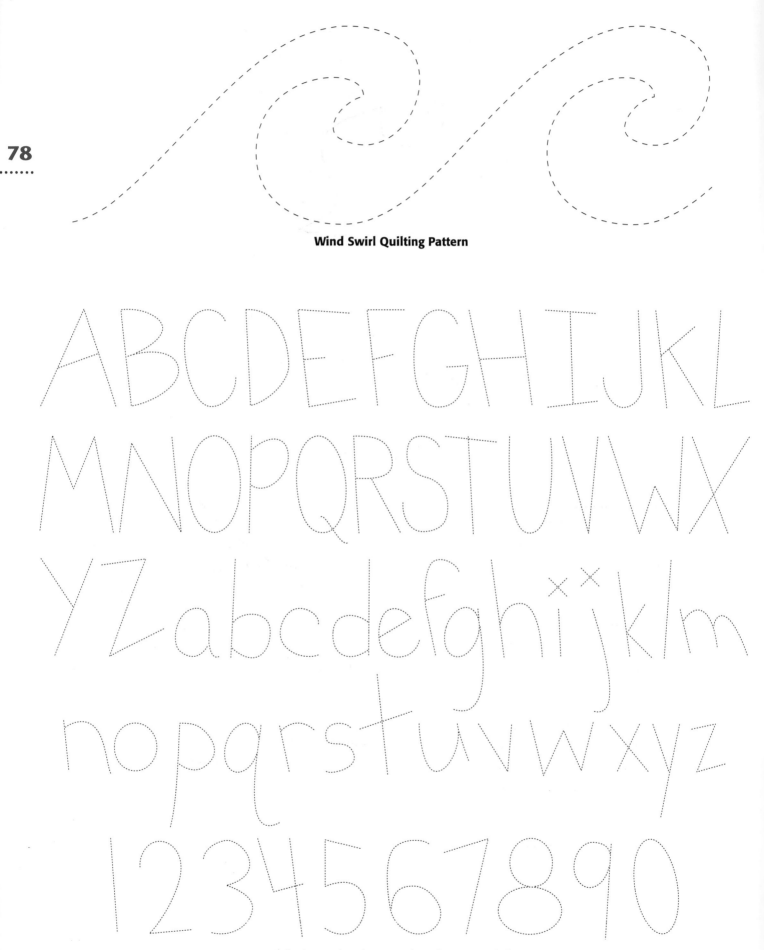

Wind Swirl Quilting Pattern

Enlarge or reduce letters and numbers as needed.

About the Author

Mary Covey is a quilter whose favorite part of the quilt process is design. She has been quilting for twenty years and has been teaching for at least fifteen of those years. Several of her designs have been published in both "Quilting Today" and "Miniature Quilts" magazines. She has won numerous awards for her miniature quilts. In 1998 she began her own quilt-pattern company called The Good Life.

When asked how she began designing and quilting, she replied, "As a child I was always volunteering to help people do things. On more than one occasion this got me into a jam. When I was twelve, I volunteered to make my own costume for the children's play at church. There was only one problem. I did not know how to sew. My mother, however, gave me some pieces of fabric and showed me how to thread her machine. I remember lying on some newspaper and having my sister trace around my body to make a pattern. I cut and sewed and sewed and cut. Two days later I had created the ugliest, most wonderful costume ever. From that day on, I was hooked on designing and sewing.

"In the early '80s, I learned to quilt and rekindled that love for designing and sewing. I've been teaching quilting for fifteen years at the same shop where I first learned to quilt—the Cotton Patch Quilt Shop."

Mary is a member of the Green Country Quilt Guild and the Itty Bitty Quilt Committee, a stitch group devoted to miniature and small quilts. She lives with her husband, John, in Jenks, a small town just outside of Tulsa, Oklahoma. She has two children, Kristi and Michael.

Martingale & Company
Toll-free: 1-800-426-3126

International: 1-425-483-3313
24-Hour Fax: 1-425-486-7596

PO Box 118, Bothell, WA 98041-0118 USA

Web site: www.patchwork.com
E-mail: info@martingale-pub.com

Books from

These books are available through your local quilt, fabric, craft-supply, or art-supply store. For more information, contact us for a free full-color catalog. You can also find our full catalog of books online at www.patchwork.com.

Appliqué
Appliqué for Baby
Appliqué in Bloom
Baltimore Bouquets
Basic Quiltmaking Techniques for Hand Appliqué
Basic Quiltmaking Techniques for Machine Appliqué
Coxcomb Quilt
The Easy Art of Appliqué
Folk Art Animals
Fun with Sunbonnet Sue
Garden Appliqué
The Nursery Rhyme Quilt
Red and Green: An Appliqué Tradition
Rose Sampler Supreme
Stars in the Garden
Sunbonnet Sue All Through the Year

Beginning Quiltmaking
Basic Quiltmaking Techniques for Borders & Bindings
Basic Quiltmaking Techniques for Curved Piecing
Basic Quiltmaking Techniques for Divided Circles
Basic Quiltmaking Techniques for Eight-Pointed Stars
Basic Quiltmaking Techniques for Hand Appliqué
Basic Quiltmaking Techniques for Machine Appliqué
Basic Quiltmaking Techniques for Strip Piecing
The Quilter's Handbook
Your First Quilt Book (or it should be!)

Crafts
15 Beads
Fabric Mosaics
Folded Fabric Fun
Making Memories

Cross-Stitch & Embroidery
Hand-Stitched Samplers from I Done My Best
Kitties to Stitch and Quilt: 15 Redwork Designs
Miniature Baltimore Album Quilts
A Silk-Ribbon Album

Designing Quilts
Color: The Quilter's Guide
Design Essentials: The Quilter's Guide
Design Your Own Quilts
Designing Quilts: The Value of Value
The Nature of Design
QuiltSkills
Sensational Settings
Surprising Designs from Traditional Quilt Blocks
Whimsies & Whynots

Holiday
Christmas Ribbonry
Easy Seasonal Wall Quilts
Favorite Christmas Quilts from That Patchwork Place
Holiday Happenings
Quilted for Christmas
Quilted for Christmas, Book IV
Special-Occasion Table Runners
Welcome to the North Pole

Home Decorating
The Home Decorator's Stamping Book
Make Room for Quilts
Special-Occasion Table Runners
Stitch & Stencil
Welcome Home: Debbie Mumm
Welcome Home: Kaffe Fassett

Knitting
Simply Beautiful Sweaters
Two Sticks and a String

Paper Arts
The Art of Handmade Paper and Collage
Grow Your Own Paper
Stamp with Style

Paper Piecing
Classic Quilts with Precise Foundation Piecing
Easy Machine Paper Piecing
Easy Mix & Match Machine Paper Piecing
Easy Paper-Pieced Keepsake Quilts
Easy Paper-Pieced Miniatures
Easy Reversible Vests
Go Wild with Quilts
Go Wild with Quilts—Again!
It's Raining Cats & Dogs
Mariner's Medallion
Needles and Notions
Paper-Pieced Curves
Paper Piecing the Seasons
A Quilter's Ark
Sewing on the Line
Show Me How to Paper Piece

Quilting & Finishing Techniques
The Border Workbook
Borders by Design
A Fine Finish
Happy Endings
Interlacing Borders
Lap Quilting Lives!
Loving Stitches
Machine Quilting Made Easy
Quilt It!
Quilting Design Sourcebook
Quilting Makes the Quilt
The Ultimate Book of Quilt Labels

Ribbonry
Christmas Ribbonry
A Passion for Ribbonry
Wedding Ribbonry

Rotary Cutting & Speed Piecing
101 Fabulous Rotary-Cut Quilts
365 Quilt Blocks a Year Perpetual Calendar
All-Star Sampler
Around the Block with Judy Hopkins
Basic Quiltmaking Techniques for Strip Piecing
Beyond Log Cabin
Block by Block
Easy Stash Quilts
Fat Quarter Quilts
The Joy of Quilting
A New Twist on Triangles
A Perfect Match
Quilters on the Go
ScrapMania
Shortcuts
Simply Scrappy Quilts
Spectacular Scraps
Square Dance
Stripples Strikes Again!
Strips That Sizzle
Surprising Designs from Traditional Quilt Blocks

Traditional Quilts with Painless Borders
Time-Crunch Quilts
Two-Color Quilts

Small & Miniature Quilts
Bunnies by the Bay Meets Little Quilts
Celebrate! With Little Quilts
Easy Paper-Pieced Miniatures
Fun with Miniature Log Cabin Blocks
Little Quilts all Through the House
Living with Little Quilts
Miniature Baltimore Album Quilts
A Silk-Ribbon Album
Small Quilts Made Easy
Small Wonders

Surface Design
Complex Cloth
Creative Marbling on Fabric
Dyes & Paints
Fantasy Fabrics
Hand-Dyed Fabric Made Easy
Jazz It Up
Machine Quilting with Decorative Threads
New Directions in Chenille
Thread Magic
Threadplay with Libby Lehman

Topics in Quiltmaking
Bargello Quilts
The Cat's Meow
Even More Quilts for Baby
Everyday Angels in Extraordinary Quilts
Fabric Collage Quilts
Fast-and-Fun Stenciled Quilts
Folk Art Quilts
It's Raining Cats & Dogs
Kitties to Stitch and Quilt: 15 Redwork Designs
Life in the Country with Country Threads
Machine-Stitched Cathedral Windows
More Quilts for Baby
A New Slant on Bargello Quilts
Patchwork Pantry
Pink Ribbon Quilts
Quilted Landscapes
The Quilted Nursery
Quilting Your Memories
Quilts for Baby
Quilts from Aunt Amy
Whimsies & Whynots

Watercolor Quilts
More Strip-Pieced Watercolor Magic
Quick Watercolor Quilts
Strip-Pieced Watercolor Magic
Watercolor Impressions
Watercolor Quilts

Wearables
Easy Reversible Vests
Just Like Mommy
New Directions in Chenille
Quick-Sew Fleece
Variations in Chenille

5/00